THE COCKNEY COMMANDO

From the mean streets of the East End of London to
one of the toughest jobs in the British Forces

Anthony Collins

THE COCKNEY COMMANDO

From the mean streets of the East End of London to one of the toughest jobs in the British Forces

MEREO

Cirencester

Published by Mereo

Mereo is an imprint of Memoirs Publishing

25 Market Place, Cirencester, Gloucestershire GL7 2NX
Tel: 01285 640485, Email: info@mereobooks.com
www.memoirspublishing.com, www.mereobooks.com

Printed in England

DEDICATION

This book is dedicated to the many wonderful people of Malta GC, many of whom went through hell in the Second World War. In particular to Marianne and her lovely Maltese family and my generous Cockney family. I have smashing memories of you all, thank you.

CHAPTER ONE

It was five thirty in the morning on the 7th September 1937 when the silence of early-morning Whitechapel was broken by the scream of a new-born baby from the hospital. A very small Cockney boy had been born to Alice Mary Collins and her husband Fred. Soon after, the Bow Bells rang out as if to welcome Tony Collins into the world.

No one knew at that time what an eventful, heart-breaking and exciting life this young lad would lead. It would be filled with drama at a time when London and its people were taking a bit of a pasting. Later in life, he was to attend his own school of hard knocks, and to tackle it with pride. The East End of London was to be the playground of hard knocks administered by others for the next fourteen years, not counting a brief interlude in Cornwall.

Brother Jim had been born three years earlier, so Tony would have a playmate, protector and source of laughs, and I might add, finance, later on. Mother Alice was going to have a tough time trying to bring up us two herberts as well as well as coping with the bombs and havoc everywhere.

From the boys' point of view, Forest Gate and later

Leyton were great areas to grow up in, but tough. Jim was a quiet, almost laid-back young man, so not a lot was heard of him - he was almost a goody goody.

One year later, sister Lavinia came along. Soon afterwards the Collins family was moved to Francis Road, Leyton, to be nearer to the school where Grandfather was the caretaker. Bombs were dropping all around Central London, so it also made sense to move a bit further east.

It appeared that I was considered the wild one in the family, although I thought I was just a well-behaved, kind young man who occasionally did silly things. For example, I would turn the old tricycle upside down while sitting on the edge of the pavement outside our house in Francis Road, the aim being to attempt an imaginary speed record for turning the pedals, thus the rear wheels to the trike, by hand power. Alas, in an effort to gain more speed and become the world champion, my hand slipped from the pedals and on to the chain, which was fairly fizzing around at the time. It took my fingers around the rear cog, which took rather a large lump out of my index finger and mashed it up a bit. I have a serious scar to this day as a reminder.

There is no record in my memory bank as to what Mum and Dad said or did at the time. I don't think I got a beating as punishment. I believe Mother was too pre-occupied with my new sister Lavinia to be concerned about me. Brother Jim was at school just across the road, no doubt keeping Grandfather Collins, the school caretaker, very busy. When Jim got home he laughed his head off at the huge bandage on my hand. He said it looked as if I was holding a lollipop.

A lot of the older boys at Jim's school would go off and follow the sound of the bombs dropping and then go looking for shrapnel the next day. I was too young to join that level of fun, but Jim went occasionally when he could get away with it, and often came back with some souvenirs.

Poor Mum, there was more to come for her.

I had this personal challenge, to scooter all the way down the long "apples and pears" from the bedrooms to the front door. Dad had made the wooden scooter at work. I tried my hardest to stay on it, bouncing down the stairs, but I invariably fell off before I was halfway down. Mum would shout at me from the back room "stop it Tony!" because obviously I was making a bit of a noise. I was determined to achieve my goal of reaching the front door, but it was taking a lot of practice and Mum was getting a bit fed up with the racket.

Dad wasn't around very much, or so it seemed, because I can't recall him telling me off. He went up to his office in London before I got up in the mornings, and by the time he got back in the evenings I was asleep again.

I suppose it must have been a boring time for me, with my brother at school and my sister too young to play my games, so what else did I have to do prior to my schooldays? Back to the scooter and to the day it all seemed to click. On this day I came down the "apples" at a fair old lick, expecting the door to stop me with a bang and maybe a bruised nose. But the door had been left open by brother Jim on his way to school. I suppose I wasn't taking much notice as I tried to psych myself up for this early morning run. Panic, as I shot over the front doorstop and straight over the kerb into the road. In those days there wasn't a lot of traffic in Francis Road, but on this day a lorry was slowing down to turn right into Johnson's building yard just up the road from our house, to make a delivery. The driver was about to turn right into the yard when this young lad with flailing arms, trying very hard to keep his balance, shot out of the front door and into the road. The poor driver had stopped the vehicle and was having a heart attack. He got out of the cab and looked under the truck, to find me bruised and grazed but laughing my head off.

Luck would have it that our family doctor, Dr Raj, lived almost opposite us, and his nurse came out to see what had happened. "Oh no, not you again!" she said, having dealt with the finger problem previously. The scene must have been reminiscent of a Tom and Jerry cartoon. Had there been a screech of brakes, the whole street would have been full of peering neighbours, but as it turned out very few people ever knew anything about the incident.

Mother knew. It seems like an eternity now, but actually it all happened very quickly. As she came out of the house I was standing beside the lorry. I left it to the driver to explain the details to her, which from my point of view he did very well, leaving out the real danger and stupidity of her son.

There were, in the eyes of the boys, great times when the bombs went over, after the sirens had given everyone a warning. An immediate trip to the air raid shelter was called for and that meant we could stay up late, or until the all-clear was given. Sometimes as the V2 rockets came into view, everyone would wait with bated breath for the engines to cut out. We boys would rush to the window to see the rockets with their trails of fire at the rear end. If the engines stopped, then Mum would get us all under the table or a bed and wait for the big bang. Luck was on the side of the Collins family throughout those dark days.

Around 1942 it was decided to evacuate areas of the East End, because London was taking one heck of a pounding. The evacuation was put into force, but I'm not sure whether it was compulsory or left up to the parents. So one day Dad came to take us up to central London, each with a small case of clothes. We said our goodbyes to Mum, not knowing that it would be the last time we would ever see her. In retrospect, we should have made more of a fuss of her. But it was all very exciting at the time. It felt like the start of a great adventure.

I'm not sure whether sister Betty had just arrived in the world, but she wasn't coming with us. Dad took us up to London and we stayed for a couple of days and nights underground in the tube station at Liverpool Street to await our turn for a steam train journey to Cornwall.

Dad went to work just round the corner in Lombard Street for a couple of hours each morning, while brother Jim looked after us. It was quite an experience playing games on the platforms and singing songs at night, only interrupted by the trains passing through the station every ten minutes or so. That's why we couldn't play football, I suppose. The trains would stop running at about nine o'clock at night, which was the signal for all to get some rest. Now the bombing overhead would commence, but we were thankful to be where we were. We were safe. Goodness only knows what chaos there was above ground.

Then one day it was time for us Collins kids to get issued with gas masks and name tags. The journey began with a trip to Waterloo Station, and Dad travelled with us to say his goodbyes before we got on the train to Cornwall. It was to be a fabulous area to be in, at a time when living in London had lots of dark days.

We arrived safely and together at Truro station. Mrs Goodwin, who was to look after us, had arranged for us to be picked up by car and taken to Polzeath, which was to be our home for the next two and a half to three years. Her house, which was almost on the beach at Polzeath Bay, was called Pentire View. Mrs Goodwin was a lovely lady. The two boys would be cared for by her and sister Lavinia was with a family just down the road. We were all to go to the same school, so we would meet up on most days.

We all soon settled into a routine and were very well looked after. We boys had lots of fun on the beach every day. Can you imagine what a delight this was for a London kid who had seen nothing other than streets and pavements? The total freedom we now had allowed us to pick up our skills at football, cricket and cliff climbing. Funnily enough, even though we were living about a hundred yards from the sea, we never did learn to swim. I put all this down to the anti-invasion barriers, which went right across the bay.

Saturday 16th June 1942 was a bad day for bruv Jim. It was a beautiful sunny morning, so it was down to the beach as normal. It was competition time between the boys, jumping off the cliff on to soft sand, to see who could jump the furthest, a line being drawn for the longest jump. I was just in front, but Jim was determined to improve his jump, so he went slightly higher up the cliff to get more elevation. He took off with a bit of a run, while still talking. "I'm going to win!" was his last comment as he landed with his tongue out. Crunch! His knees hit his chin on impact with the ground and his teeth went straight through his tongue. There was blood everywhere.

Jim was lucky that the local GP was at home, and he managed to stem the flow of blood. It stopped Jim from talking for a week, after which he was OK. I think his teacher accused him of doing it on purpose so as to have time off from school. In a way I was pleased that I was not the only one to get into trouble. I think I almost had a smile on my face, as if I would.

While the sun was shining in Polzeath, for the next two years life was fun. The old boy, Mr Crouch, our local beachcomber, was often on the beach at the same time as us. He used to moan because our cricket pitch disturbed his flotsam and jetsam and made it hard for him to find things. We used to take the mickey out of him and that got him angry, so he would often chase us around the beach, but he was no match for us. Soon he would calm down and all would be well. What we couldn't understand was that he worked in the car showrooms in Polzeath. Why on earth there was a car showroom when there were only a couple of dozen adults in the bay? It didn't make a lot of sense.

One day we got the shocking news that Mum had passed away soon after the birth of sister Betty. How we reacted to this I don't quite know, but I seem to remember saying to myself "How could Mum do this to us at a time like this?" It just didn't seem real from where we were.

We hadn't missed London. We were very well looked after and were developing into young men physically and mentally. All the exercising on the beach was doing us a lot of good, so this was one of the obvious benefits that came out of the evacuation. I couldn't see us getting as fit as this in the back streets of the East End. The sporting skills we were developing would stand us in good stead in the future, but only time would tell.

Time in fact was going by very quickly, and we lost touch with the war effort because we were away from it.

From time to time Jim and I would climb our way up the cliffs towards Pentire Point, which overlooked St Georges Channel bordering on the Atlantic Ocean. It could get quite rough up high at Pentire, but we had great days out.

Now up until very recently I always believed that there was a castle on the end of the point. I don't know why I thought this, but over the years, in my sleep and in my dreams, there was always a castle on the point.

Betty, our sister, had now joined us at Polzeath and she went to join Lavinia in her family home. Dad and our mother's brother Uncle Jim came down with Betty and stayed for a couple of days. It was nice to see them, as well as have them play beach cricket with us. Parents in those days never talked about personal things. We never learned anything about the loss of Mum, and we never asked.

Dad told us that the war was coming to an end and that we would be going back to London in the near future. But he was very happy that we were being well looked after.

Neither Jim nor I really wanted to go back. We had mixed feelings about it all. We were old enough now to consider all the facts, and we couldn't see what our future would be, with Dad on his own and no family unit to join. We were very happy doing the things we were doing and enjoying the life we had. But the choice was not ours, and before long the return journey was upon us. More farewells and lots of 'thank yous' to the Polzeath people.

CHAPTER TWO

The journey back to London was filled with excitement, along with some fear of the unknown. It would be lovely to see all the uncles and aunties in the Mile End - Aunty Doll (Mum's sister), Uncle Pat, her husband, and Aunty Vera (Mum's other sister). They were all real Cockney people, full of generosity and humour.

Of course, all this was on the assumption that they had not been bombed out. We hadn't heard anything, so I assumed all was well, but we would soon find out. I wondered if anybody was going to meet us at Waterloo Station. Of course there were four of us now; Jim was eleven, I was eight, Lavinia was six and a half and Betty was still only three years old.

As it turned out, Dad was waiting at the station. We wondered what his plans were for us all. A foster home, or even an orphanage? Or was he going to try to manage on his own?

There were a lot of children getting off the train at Waterloo, so it was a mass return to 'normality'. It's very strange that at the time you as individuals believe that this is only happening to you, but looking at all the kids I wonder just how much tragedy was going to come out in the lives of all these youngsters. Hitler had a lot to answer for.

Dad had arranged for us all to go to Aldersbrook Homes, a sort of orphanage in Wanstead. He said at the time that it was the best he could do. I suppose he did have a private life, but I felt his responsibilities were now towards his children.

So it was going to be an institutional life for us all. Dad apparently was attempting to find an alternative, but without a mother there wasn't a lot of hope.

I suppose really what kept us, or at least the boys, going was the thought of the sports programme which was an integral part of the orphanage lifestyle. They had two soccer pitches, a lovely cricket pitch, which could have been the envy of many county grounds, and indoor facilities for badminton and squash.

As a bonus for us, Dad became a part-time sports master for the orphanage, so we saw quite a lot of him. Being in an institution, discipline was of the essence. It didn't do us much harm and was to prove very helpful in our careers in the future. Once again we spent a lot of time playing various sports, and I believe this is what kept us out of more trouble. Of course I was no angel and was always looking for adventure and something new to do.

One day Jim and I decided to go adventure camping in the forest about a mile away from the orphanage. We managed to scrounge some eggs and sausages from one of the kind canteen staff. Off we went to a part of Epping Forest which we knew was used as a hideout and camp for those who needed to use it. When we got there, in the bushes were some house bricks and sheet metal. We were on our own, so we made a sort of cooker with the bricks and used the sheet metal as the hot plate. We got a fire going and were quite comfortable.

We decided to do a bit of tree climbing to work up an appetite, then settled down to cook a meal. I must admit that it wasn't very hygienic, but it tasted good. It was spoilt by having no bread. The sarnies were out. But for us it was great fun to get away from the institute for a short while.

About mid-afternoon we started to tidy up before making our way back, but not before we made sure that the fire was out. We dispersed the bricks, and off we set back to our residence.

We had got about half a mile from the wooded camp site when we heard the sound of fire engines coming up the road, heading for the area we had just left. We dared not go back. We could only assume that the hot bricks had reignited something.

After about twelve months in the orphanage, Dad managed to find a lady who was prepared not only to marry him but to take on us four children, a task that could be considered to be traumatic and full of danger for any woman to take on. She was a lady by the name of Edith, who owned a small grocery shop in Francis Road. She also had a daughter by her first marriage, Doreen, who was married to a wartime Royal Marine by the name of Ron. So we all moved into a very small downstairs flat in Leyton. It was always going to be difficult for size - so many people having to live in harmony in such a small area.

The place consisted of two bedrooms, a front room, a

dining room and a very small kitchen. There was an outside loo, but no bathroom. There was a tin bath hanging on the wall outside the back door. The two girls had a pull-down bed in the front room, stepmum and dad had the middle bedroom and Jim and I shared a bed in the back room. I could see there was going to be lots of laughs, some stupidity, lots of punishments and a fair amount of growing up.

Initially all was well, and it appeared everyone was happy. Dad would go off to work in London, we four would go to school and stepmum Edith would open her shop at about 9 am each morning.

Friday nights would be bath nights. The big tin bath would be brought in from out back, for the children only. I think Dad had a bath or shower at the Royal Insurance Company office in Lombard Street, while our stepmum would have her bath when we were at school, or maybe in the flat above the shop.

But back to us. The girls went first, I suppose because they were considered to be the cleanest and of course the youngest. The big battle was between Jim and me, because the water was getting colder by the minute and for whoever went last, poor soul, the water was getting dirtier as well. Once we were done we would have to carry the bath outside the back door, scrub it down and empty it down the drain. Trying to get the water actually down the drain was an art, as most of it ended up going down the garden. The last ritual was to dry the bath and hang it back up on the wall.

For me the one good thing that came out of that bath was the fact that we knew there was no school the next day. That meant we would probably play football, if allowed, on the Saturday, only to get covered in mud. If we were playing for the school or the orphanage - we still played for them - at least we could get a shower after the game.

As teenagers my brother and I would spend a lot of time playing in the street outside our house in Richmond Road, Leytonstone. At the time there were hardly any cars on the roads, so we were able to play all kinds of games in the street. There were lots of boys of our age. John and Roy Ellis were opposite and further down the road the Brierleys and Taylors lived, all school chums.

Football was not played very much in the street, being reserved for the school playground. But it just so happened that the trees in our road were about twenty yards apart, just about right for a cricket pitch. The stumps were painted on the tree trunk and the crease was one pavement slab from the tree. Although we were hemmed in on both sides by houses, which restricted the cut and hook, the straight drive down the road was great for scoring runs. A soft ball was always used, so not many windows got broken and few balls were lost. Anyway, the neighbours always knew who was playing.

Pads, gloves and helmets were never required, though bouncers were the order of the day from the bowler and we became skilled at dealing with them. Keeping your eye on the ball because you knew it was soft was a great aid to

My father

Our lovely mum

AC's mum, her brother uncle Jim
and sisters, aunty Doll and aunty Vera

AC at about nine months

AC with sister Lavinia and brother Jimmy, just arrived in Cornwall

1946 - the Collins children just after Dad got remarried

Newport School, 1949

Newport School team, 1948.
Went on to be the 1949 champs.

The Collins children
in about 1949/50

T Collins (wicketkeeper) centre front row, about 1950

The orphanage soccer team, 1952 – TC 2nd left front row,
Mr Collins top left

Lost our lovely mum. The reason why we are at the orphanage

good batting. As a bowler, moving a soft, seamless ball in the air, became quite an art. The bat was generally made out of an old piece of wood, although occasionally someone got a real bat as a gift for a birthday or Christmas.

The games were very competitive and a lot of fun. I can remember running for a catch, a very high catch. Head up, eyes on the ball and full of concentration, I ran straight in to a tree. There is something about my nose that seems to like getting in the way.

One of the boys' favourite pastimes was roller skating. The roads were very smooth, having been re-tarmacked after the war, and with little or no traffic it was relatively safe. The biggest danger was the skates themselves, which had clamps at the front to fit over the soles of your shoes, with straps around the ankles. If the skates were too big or small it was very hard to secure them to your shoes. It was a nightmare if you came off, which often happened when travelling at speed. You were in for a tumble unless you could manage to maintain a balancing act on one foot until you came to a stop.

Surprisingly we were able to become quite good at reverse skating, turning at speed and jumping over obstacles, but our toecaps and trouser knees did take a pounding.

Levels of skill at all sports in our street and at our schools were very high. Though we were mainly self-taught, we had hours and hours of practice, I suppose because we had nothing else to do. Great times.

Grandfather Collins would march up the road at about the same time every day, heading towards his house in Chertsey Road, where he had moved after his retirement from the school caretaker's job. I can never remember him stopping to call in to speak to us children, somewhat different in attitude from grandparents of today. But we as children knew very little about our grandparents. I later found out that there were many secrets in the family, most of which were associated with them.

I think I have mentioned that Dad's sister, Aunty Ivy, lived just round the corner from us, with her husband Alf and son Roy. Uncle Alf was a baker's delivery man, delivering bread in a lorry to the local shops in Leyton, Leytonstone and the surrounding area. In fact he gave me a job on Saturdays helping him to deliver. I think it was to help him to get back in time for the football at West Ham or Leyton Orient.

Aunty Ivy was always interested in the Collins kids. I think she was much closer to our Dad than she was to her other brothers and sisters. That was the impression we got, perhaps because we saw more of her. As far as I was concerned Grandfather John Collins was a mystery man, as were his two wives – or was it three?

As far as our schooling went, I was at Newport Road School with our sisters and Jim was at Norlington Road School for Boys. Both schools were very keen on their sports and their achievements.

As it turned out, both of us boys succeeded in achieving the captaincy of the school soccer and cricket teams. Jim was a very good footballer, though competition at his school was exceptional. Jerry Ward, who went on to England Schoolboys, and Jim himself went on to captain the British Army team at a time when the army was full of professional footballers who were doing their National Service.

I was very much more adept at cricket. I joined Jim at Norlington at a time when he only had one year left before reaching the age of fifteen, the age to join the big world of the employed. Later on in life I was to find out that Graham Gooch, England cricket captain, the TV presenter Jonathan Ross and the Arsenal footballer Vic Groves all went to Norlington Road school - much later of course.

In the meantime Jim was able to give me some protection as my big brother. He taught me how to look after myself and how to take care of the bullies. In those days you dealt with them yourself, in your own way. Mind you those situations were considered to be character building and good for you.

My brother would also finance my love of broken biscuits and crisps, which one of us purchased from the local shop on the corner on the way to school. As a matter of interest, Dad's sister Aunty Ivy lived just down the road from the shop and she would often look out for us as we went by.

Poor Jim really did suffer for having a younger brother, especially one who was considered by the Collins side of the family as the good one, because he occasionally wet the bed. It was one of the penalties of living in a small cramped house with the loo outside in the garden - that was my excuse.

There again I would often get accused by my stepmother of doing things I hadn't done, because she was a little afraid of Jim since he had grown into a big lad. I know I could not be classed as an angel, but I used to take many a punishment from our stepmother for things I never did. One of the most frustrating things in life is being blamed for doing something you know you haven't done.

I can remember distinctly one situation in particular at home in Leyton. It was just before Christmas and stepmum had apparently found a bargain somewhere in one of the markets. It was a very large box of chocolates, well suited for a family Christmas. She decided to hide the box from prying eyes, and chose to hide it under the stairs. There was an old coal cupboard and built in to the wall was a small recess, big enough to take the box. Obviously she then forgot about it. As we got to Christmas she couldn't find the chocolates and accused me, in front of the other kids, of taking it to school to share with my mates. I denied it, and got a bashing. Every time she accused me, I denied it again and got another bashing. This went on for a week or so.

Jim had faith in me because he knew that if I had taken them I would have told him. Just after Christmas he decided to search the house when stepmother wasn't around. He found them, and confronted her with them. Even then she didn't back down but accused us of hiding the box. No apology, nothing. That has stuck with me to this day.

Then it was time for Jim to leave school and very soon

after, to leave home and join the big world. When this happened we lost contact with him for some time.

I had a couple more years to serve at school and for some reason I realized that I had better knuckle down and get a bit of an education. Sport wasn't going to be everything. My school reports were reasonable. I was always mid position in class and almost top at physical training.

I began to work harder at lessons and didn't have the blackboard rubber thrown at me so often. The visits to the headmaster were becoming less frequent, as reflected in my school reports, which pleased Dad. Well, he had to sign the reports, I presume after reading them.

For some reason sister Lavinia left home to live with Aunty Doll in Bow.

Dad went to work in London every working day, normally before the two remaining children got up, although I could hear him pottering around washing and shaving. He was beginning to cough and splutter a lot, no doubt as a result of smoking and the tough stressful life he had led so far. When he came home in the evening he was always very quiet. He never told us off or went against anything Edith said. He was obviously very thankful for the role she had played in rearing his family during a difficult period of his life.

Edith in the meantime had found it difficult to run the shop and the home. I assume she sold it, for she never went back to it after Lavinia left. It was certainly a lot quieter in the house, with much more room.

I started my own paper round at a shop at the top of

Francis Road, which meant getting up much earlier so that I could finish the round before school. I enjoyed the round very much, because it gave me more financial and cultural independence. I had a little money in my pocket, which was a great feeling. I no longer had to run the three miles to Eton Manor to play football for my school. If I did, at least I could come back on the bus.

One weekend there was a fair at the Green Man in Leytonstone, and with a little money in my pocket I went along. At the shooting gallery I spent a shilling, which gave me two or three goes. I found that I was a reasonable shot and won a Wedgwood dinner plate. It was only a second from the manufacturer, but it gave me great deal of pleasure to present it to my stepmother. She didn't really appreciate it or show any signs of a "thank you" or "well done". I have the plate at home now, sixty years on.

I was looking forward to finishing school, but I had to be patient and let time go by naturally, without wishing my life away too quickly.

Life at home settled down to a more sedate routine with just two of us. I wasn't out in the street so much playing games. Maybe I was just growing up.

Then one day Dad came home from work and told me he had two options for me with regard to future work. The first was to do an apprenticeship as an electrician in London. I believe Dad would have liked me to take that option, as we could have travelled to the city together. The alternative was to go to Braintree Agricultural College to learn farming.

I had a few months to think it over, but I knew what my choice was going to be. The outdoor life was appealing to me straight away.

First I had a bit more work to do at school. I was working very hard in the classroom. For some reason I was very good at arithmetic, especially mental arithmetic. I put this down to the times table, which I had learned parrot fashion at a very early stage. I was very quick off the mark when asked by the teacher to solve a mathematical problem. My final report from the school was reasonable and I thought that it would always help me, should anyone ask to see it.

The year was now 1952, Coronation year, and an apprentice farmer was about to be let loose. It was time to say goodbye to my stepmum and Dad and to set off on a journey which I hoped was going to be a lot of fun.

CHAPTER THREE

A young man setting off at the age of fifteen years can find some fun in most situations - as I was to find out later, even in desperate ones. Getting freedom from home restrictions was a very good start to getting some happiness and joy put back into my life, but there was no guarantee that everything would work out in my favour.

I arrived at the college just outside Braintree to find that it was housed in a magnificent manor house with its own land. I was soon settled into my room and introduced to the staff and other pupils. Some of the students had been there some time, so they knew the routine, which was a great help to me.

The early days at the college were to prove very demanding, as we had to rise at 4 am and venture out into the bitter cold. Even so I loved the animal husbandry, milking, feeding systems and bringing calves and piglets into the world. I enjoyed finding out how horses tick and how (almost) to control them, crop rotation and the general scheme of running a farm. I really loved the art of hedge-cutting and laying.

It was in my first year at the college that I had to learn to shave, and before breakfast as well. As the summer approached, farm work got physically very much harder. Haymaking and harvesting certainly strengthened the back muscles. There was heavy lifting of straw and hay bales or two-and-a-half hundredweight bags of corn, and we had to build silage pits. It was very hard, but extremely rewarding and happy work.

At the end of the day there wasn't a lot of time for socialising, and tiredness generally got the better of even young bodies. But country life was turning out to be brilliant. Rabbit hunting with ferrets and shotgun often put a meal on the table at weekends. The cricket season took priority in summer and the local village team was made up the farming community.

After a year at the college, students would be taken on by local farmers to work on their farms, which increased our knowledge of general farm management. It was a bit like a cattle market. I was offered to a Mr Hughes, who had a 200-acre farm in the village of Great Sampford in Essex. Yet another move was imminent.

It was a good job I didn't have many possessions, as this move meant going into lodgings. I was hoping that Mr Hughes had taken care of all that, and he had, because when I arrived at the farm mid-morning, he was there to introduce me to his senior farm worker, Fred. Fred took me to the farmhouse, where his wife, Mrs Thomas, was waiting to greet me. They were quite elderly but appeared to be very nice people. I supposed it would be good for them to have a young person around.

Fred, being the farm supervisor, would give me my

work schedule on a daily basis. He took me round the farm and I met the two other members of staff. John was Fred's son and the tractor driver, Brian was the dairyman and in addition there was a very old man, George, who worked part-time hedging and hoeing in the sugar beet season. It appeared that Mr Hughes was a gentleman farmer who did very little work on the farm himself.

Later that day Mrs Thomas baked a lovely pigeon pie. She was a very good cook, as I suppose most countrywomen are - and have to be. They had a very large garden where all the vegetables were grown, plus half a dozen chickens. Of course from the land they could get rabbits, pheasants, pigeons and hares. The milk from the dairy could not have been fresher, and occasionally the odd pig would not go amiss. All in all I could see a lot going for this sort of life, though winter was yet to come.

My little room upstairs was comfortable and cosy, but I did need a radio to keep up to date with world events. Radio Caroline had just begun to push out current popular music, so I thought of ringing Dad to ask him to get me a radio. He beat me to it, because the college had told him where I had been sent. He rang to tell me that Jim had joined the army and had got married to Jean. The army bit was a surprise to me, because he had never shown any interest in the military. He was now serving in Egypt.

I told Dad that I was very happy on the farm, although the work was hard. I must admit that Dad sounded much chirpier now that the flock had flown. But parents never mentioned such things then.

Fred assigned me to the dairy side initially, to work with Brian and the fifty cows, milking early mornings because I lived on the farm. This gave Brian a little leeway because if he was slightly late turning up I would already have got things under way. I would go up to the top field and call the cows in for milking. They were always keen to come to parlour because of the good-tasting food they got there as a supplement to their diet, and the relief of getting rid of all that milk.

First thing in the morning on my way up to the top field, I would nip in to the dairy and scrape the cream off the top of the churn. It was lovely. After milking it was back to the house, where Mrs Thomas would rustle up a nice fried breakfast. I would then join Fred and his son for the daily tasks, which would vary from day to day according to the farming season.

I was taught to drive a tractor and allowed to do so on the farm property. There was one carthorse, a Shire, on the farm and seemingly Fred was the only one who could handle it safely, so he took that responsibility. John was a skilled tractor driver and he would carry out the ploughing and sowing etc, while I was allowed to do the raking and rolling (no, it wasn't a new dance!)

Fred was extremely skilful at building haystacks and corn stacks. This was the period just before the introduction of balers and combines, so haystacks were still being built. I learned a lot very quickly about farming in my first year at the Hughes farm.

Poor Mrs Thomas was not in the best of health, so I

was soon asked to look for alternative lodgings. I didn't want to but needs must.

Fred would occasionally go down to the local pub, the Bull, in the evenings. One day he came back with the news that the owners of the local grocer's shop, Mr and Mrs Woods, were prepared to have a lodger. They had two boys about my age, David and Bill, who by chance were cricketers, and they were keen to have me along. Their shop was about one and a half miles from the farm, which meant that if I wanted to live there I would need some form of transport to get to work.

The following day I went down to the village to introduce myself to the Wood family. We seemed to get on very well. I mentioned to them about getting a bicycle and Mr Woods suggested that we go straight down to the other side of the village to Mr Moore's hardware shop.

I met 'Pony' Moore, the son, while waiting to talk to his father, who had another customer at the time. I liked Pony, having met him briefly before in the village. He was a good sportsman and a quiet lad, which suited me. Two of a kind I suppose.

After I got my bicycle we did a lot of travelling around at weekends when not required on the farm. Pony's parents had a tennis court in their front garden, so Pony and I spent some time practising.

Back to business. I ended up purchasing, on the 'never-never', a gleaming new Raleigh Roadster with three-speed gears. I was to pay five shillings a week to a total of £17, about a year in payments. I paid a pound a week to Mrs

Woods for my accommodation, leaving me about five shillings pocket money - not bad really, for that time.

I agreed with Mrs Woods that I would join them the following weekend. She said she was looking looked forward to my stay. I went back to the farm to tell Fred and his wife and Mr Hughes of the plan.

The winter period on the farm varied between very harsh and impossible according to the weather conditions. The cattle we brought in to the barn for warmth and safety. The pigs were already under cover and the chickens were housed in separate cages under cover. In the fields the sugar beet was ready to be topped and tailed and put into heaps ready to be forked on to the tractor and trailer. The forks used were like a standard garden fork but much bigger, with metal balls on the points to stop the fork from piercing the sugar beets, which were like large turnips. Each load of beet was taken to the outdoor silo and covered with straw to keep off the snow and frost. Later, in the early part of the new year, the beet would be transported to the Tate & Lyle sugar factory in Dunmow.

If the weather was really bad we would turn our hand to hedging. The art of laying a hedge has to be taught to you by an expert. Old George was just that person, with many years of experience. He showed me how to cut without damaging each individual branch, so that the growth continued. You had to lay it neatly and level so that the finished article looked aesthetically professional. One great attraction of winter hedging was the huge bonfire that went with the job.

I spent Christmas with the Wood family, which was great because they could afford to celebrate in a fairly big way, with all the trimmings. There was very little time off from work because animals do not stop wanting at Christmas time, their needs are ongoing. Once the festive period has gone then you can start thinking about spring and summer and of course the cricket season and all that goes with that.

The news I had about Jim reminded me of a photo of Ron in the hall at home in Leyton. He was in uniform, and that set my mind in motion. I was now seventeen years of age, almost six feet tall and very fit from the farm work. There were times when I was alone when I would take stock of my life and wonder whether farming was the right role for me, much as I loved it. However I can say with some certainty that I was very happy with life at that time. I had excelled in the local cricket league the previous season and had learned to drive. The people around me were lovely, and it was great living in the village enjoying the local community life. Was there anything missing from the village? Romance, perhaps.

My introduction to girls, or should I say a girl, really was a first. It was a lovely sunny midsummer Sunday, and we had a cricket match at home in Thaxted. I had been selected with the Wood boys to play. I decided to cycle to the game, while the Woods went in the family car because mother Wood had made the sandwiches and cakes for the teams. I set off after Sunday lunch to ride the three miles to Thaxted, my cricket gear following with the Wood brothers.

It was a great game. We lost to Saffron Walden, but it was close. I had a reasonable game behind the stumps. At the interval a local girl called Shirley asked if she could cycle back to Sampford with me after the game. My initial thoughts were that Pony Moore had set me up. I never thought any more about it during the final session of the game. She was waiting for me to get changed after the game, so I made sure I had a shower.

We set of on a slow ride back to the village. It was an easy ride back, because most of the route was downhill. As we cycled along I thought to myself that this was something totally new to me. I had seen this girl in the village occasionally, but I didn't know her at all. What should I talk about? I didn't want to appear as the London city boy who knew it all, because I didn't. I really was shy and totally lacking in experience. I don't know why, but I felt she was also new at relationships.

I managed to ask her a few questions about herself and slowly the ice was broken, though there were still a number of silences. We seemed to be getting on quite well, with a few laughs here and there, which always helps a situation.

The road back from Thaxted was very much country lanes, no shops or houses, just farmland. She suggested that we stop for a drink, and she had the orangeade. We pulled into a cornfield and parked our bikes just inside the gate. We sat down on the edge of the corn, and it was at this point that I realised I really didn't know anything about romance and courting. I didn't spot any signals, assuming some were given. Looking back on the scene, it really was idyllic for a first-time encounter. Sitting close to a young lady for the first time was great, she smelled fresh and very nice. I must admit that I felt like giving her a hug, but I didn't think it would be right. I just held her hand to get her back up to her feet as we started home.

Looking back over the years, the boys of the 1950s had a lot of respect for young ladies and tended to treat them in that way. The girls themselves expected to have respect and to be treated like ladies and accordingly they behaved more like them. Getting involved with girls seemed to start at a very much later point in a boy's life. The combination of respect and involvement was no bad thing, in my view.

I think my attitude must have impressed her, because she said that it had been nice and maybe we could meet again. The rest of the journey was very pleasant. I escorted her to her mother's bungalow on the edge of the village. I said thank you and goodbye at the gate with no further arrangements.

That evening in my room at Mrs Woods', I once again started thinking about my future. Did I want to stay here in the village, working on the farm, getting more involved with the village people and activities on a very low wage, with as far as I could see very few prospects of bettering myself? Only time would tell. The decision was going to have to be mine.

The earliest I could join the forces was at eighteen years of age. I was really enjoying my work on the farm, living in the village and earning the recognition of the local people, especially when I was involved with sports. Maybe it was the shyness of the London lad that attracted the attention of the locals.

Then a local farmer's daughter brought her dad along to Thaxted to watch a cricket match - allegedly. An invitation to a game of tennis at their place was the outcome. Pony Moore was with me at the time, so I asked her dad if Pony could come along with me as he was a reasonable tennis player. He approved of that, and said a four would be fine. Immediately, in my mind, I turned the game into a tournament, which was fixed for the following weekend.

When I told Mr Wood of the arrangement he couldn't believe what I was saying. The gentleman in question was a real squire of the manor and didn't often give out invitations to the locals.

We did have a lovely Saturday afternoon. The farm house was magnificent. It was a manor house, with the tennis court at the end of the drive. I asked Pony if he had known this place was here and he just nodded with a smile. I wondered if we should go round the back, tradesman's entrance you know, us on bikes.

They must have seen us coming down the drive, because they came out together. He introduced himself as Peter Taylor and his daughter as Brenda. I was very pleased I had decided to wear my cricket whites, because at least I didn't feel out of place from that point of view.

We had a smashing (excuse the pun) afternoon of tennis, changing partners every so often so that the conversation didn't get too boring and to balance out the games. Pony and I played very well and were quite strong and forceful. I did mention to Pony that we should rein back a little as guests and not be over aggressive. I think Mr Taylor recognised that what we had done was to the benefit of his daughter and the afternoon's sport.

We had a lovely tea, with real country cakes. During tea I mentioned to Peter that I was thinking of joining the Royal Marines in the New Year. This got him talking about his naval career in the last war. He had been a commander, no less, and of course he knew a lot about the Royals, as he called them.

If I had been going to stay in the village, the tennis sessions might have become a regular event - who knows? Anyway the day was great and I think it opened Pony's eyes to a broader social level. Going back to work on the Monday morning brought me back to earth with a bump.

That week back on the farm, I helped to bring a couple of calves into the world. It surprised me just how tough you had to be as a 'midwife' to cattle. Quite often there were difficulties with the calf's front feet being in the wrong place. The head was sometimes facing backwards and I was told the calf was back to front. In this case the mother would not have calved naturally without human help. We even had to use ropes attached to tractors at times. But it was great when the youngsters were born safely. I can't remember losing one, but there were many tough times.

The piglets seem to birth a lot easier, I think because they were multiple births, eight, ten or even twelve. The piglets were gorgeous and the mothers were so placid during and after giving birth.

For me this was a wonderful experience and it was at times like this that thoughts of giving it up for the military raised doubts in my mind. Then on the other hand I would think about working in the fields in the heart of winter, and the pay structure. I had a difficult decision to make.

As I cycled to work the next day at five o'clock, I made my decision. I decided that I would apply to join the Royal Marines. My application meant that I would have to travel to London for the interview at the recruiting office.

The Royal Marines being an élite corps, you had to put your case for joining with some sincerity. Although at that time in 1955 many who had served in the war had left the service and there were a number of vacancies, you still had to make a burly sergeant want you to join. The standard was not going to be lowered just to meet recruiting levels.

I did my best at the interview and very much hoped I would be accepted. Maybe the fact that brother Jim was in the army might help a little. The sergeant said I would be informed by letter in about ten days' time. On the train back to Saffron Walden I still had some doubts as to whether I was doing the right thing; only time would tell. I had made the decision, and if selected I would give it my all. So that was it.

I hoped that I had done enough at the interview and maybe my sporting record would help. I thought perhaps Jim's career might be influential and the fact that I could drive might be a help to them in making their decision. I just had to wait and see.

In the meantime it was back to the village to await the outcome. I informed Mr Hughes of my intentions in case I had to give in my notice suddenly. Everyone was asking how I got on at the interview, but of course I couldn't give them a real answer, only tell them how I felt I had done. I was surprised to see how much interest was shown. If it happened, this was going to be the hardest farewell so far.

The next few days were full of apprehension. Every time I saw Joe the postman cycling around the village, I wondered if he was going to call me over, but not so far. I tried to continue my life as normal, working as usual but rushing to get home in the evening to see if the postman had been. I was eighteen in September 1955, the interview had taken place in October of that year and January 1956 would be the intake date if I was successful.

One Thursday morning in late October while I was at work, an official-looking brown envelope marked "HM Service" arrived at the shop. Mr Wood, bless him, decided that it looked important enough for him to drive to the farm with it. It was never going to be easy for him to find me in 200 acres of land, because there wasn't anybody in the yard for him to ask, but as luck would have it, Fred was going back to the stables with the Shire horse, which I think had gone a bit lame or needed a shoe. He saw Mr Wood in the yard and told him where I was working. As soon as I saw Mr Wood trudging up the path towards the hedge I was working on, I knew this was the moment I had been waiting for so impatiently.

To my delight, the brown envelope contained a congratulatory letter with all the instructions for joining. Mr Wood smiled and said "well done", and I thanked him for going to all the trouble of finding me. At the end of the day's work I gave in my notice to Mr Hughes and thanked him for all of his help. What I saw in his face led me to believe that because he didn't have any children of his own, he looked upon me almost as one of his own. Who knows what the future might have brought if I had stayed? But I couldn't dwell on that thought.

In the next few weeks building up to Christmas and the New Year, there seemed to be a constant round of farewells. There were many lovely people in the village who had helped to shape my life and character over the past two years. I gave my trusted Raleigh roadster to Pony Moore so that he could make a few shillings in his dad's shop.

It really was a sad time for me. I didn't even know if I would ever see these lovely people again, ever. But at least I was joining the forces with a decent set of cricket whites and a pair of pigskin boots - a wonderful reminder of good times.

CHAPTER FOUR

The train journey to Deal gave me plenty of time to think, and I know that sometimes that can be dangerous. Sitting in the carriage on my own, for some reason I began to analyse my character. Was I mentally strong enough? I was full of trepidation and fear that I was going to fail at this enormous task I was asking myself to fulfil.

As I have said before, I am by nature a very quiet person, introverted and very much a loner. I enjoy my own company and feel slightly uncomfortable in the presence of my elders. Up until now this had not been very much of a hindrance, because I had not been involved with a real challenge in life, but what I was going to do next was going to test me and my character. I was a little afraid, but on the positive side I knew that when I was on the sports field I was a different, more confident person.

So what was that telling me? I believed I would not be able to change my character overnight, and I couldn't just believe I was good at everything, because I would soon be shot down by the other blokes around me. What I did sincerely believe is that if you know you are good, even very good, at something, it does not matter how many people are watching you, you will always give an impression of confidence and you will feel confident. A shining example of this was at Peter Taylor's manor on the tennis court.

I decided I would give 100% effort to make myself good at whatever I was told to do; then it would be much easier mentally and physically to succeed.

While thinking about all this, I fell asleep and began dreaming. I woke up feeling much more confident in what I was about to do.

Apparently there were forty other young men joining 650 Squad at Deal on that day and two other young lads had joined me in the carriage while I was asleep. I thought I recognised one of them as Tony Gubby, a student at Braintree College. He had made the same decision as I had and was taking the ultimate challenge, for the same reasons as myself.

Now the story really unfolds. The train pulled into Deal station and we gathered the one suitcase that was allowed and piled off the train. I didn't know what to expect next - perhaps it was going to be an initiative test to find our way to the barracks. But suddenly a voice bellowed out "fall in over here you lot!"

Corporal Hutton was there to greet us. It appeared that the station wasn't very far from the barracks, so it was a right turn, quick march to the East Wing of Deal Barracks. The barber's shop was conveniently sited just inside the gate, and in alphabetical order a short back and sides was the order of the day for everyone. No one left the scene until the whole intake had been shorn of their locks.

Once we were fallen in, it was a short march to the lecture room, where the Adjutant and Sergeant Major were waiting to greet us in their own inimitable way. The reason for this get-together was for them to introduce themselves, which was never to be forgotten, and to lay down the ground rules. They also presented everyone with the traditional Queen's Shilling, now that we had signed on the dotted line for whatever number of years we had chosen. I had signed for seven years, with five on the reserves. This was to change later. Once signed it meant that there was no way out, and the discipline and regulations began from that moment on. Now there were no excuses. You were expected to know right from wrong.

We were introduced to the adjutant (Capt Morgan) the Sergeant Major (CSM Brierley) the squad sergeant (Sgt Tyack) and the squad corporal we had already met. There was one other, the Physical Training Instructor (Sgt Jones).

It was time to be taken to our barrack accommodation room to be issued with our beds, bedding and lockers. On the wall was a printed list of the daily cleaning duties. "Learn them!" said Cpl Hutton, before falling us in for a marched tour of the barracks. He pointed out the dhoby room, showers and 'heads' (toilets) before moving on to the gymnasium and the galley, both of which were to play a big part in our lives in the next twelve weeks.

When it was confirmed that all the trains for the day had arrived and all forty men had turned up and had gone through the ritual, it was time to be issued with every conceivable item of kit. At this stage some of the items were totally baffling. Everything went into our large khaki kitbags and small green kitbags.

Boots and webbing would need a lot of work. Webbing for Royal Marines went from khaki, as issued, to highly-polished black for everyday use and white for ceremonial parades. As it turned out, some of the items that were issued would never be used, for example brown Jesus sandals and thick fleece underwear.

With all the kit over our shoulders, the next stop on our way back to the barrack room was at the NAAFI for tins of black boot polish, Brasso, dusters, personal items like soap, toothpaste and dhobi powder (for clothes washing). From what I could see with this lot, the next month was going to be a real learning curve. We would have to learn about military jargon, and most of that would have to come from our instructors and from other lads who had joined earlier and were in the 649 squad and the band service. 'Heads' (toilets), 'yomping' (cross-country travel on foot) and 'scran' (food) were just a few to start with.

Our real first names were hardly ever used, because nearly every surname had a nickname to go with it. For example, all Woods were Timber, Whites were Chalky (even if you were black), Bells were Dinger, Murphys were Spuds and Collinses were Jumper. So it went on.

It had been a very long day and I was beginning to wilt. I hoped the Sergeant Major was going to be kind to us all on day one and give us a chance to get a good night's sleep. One thing was for sure, all our items of kit had to be folded away into our lockers.

We had to go and read company orders to see what our routine was for tomorrow. One thing Cpl Hutton impressed upon us was never, ever, to miss reading company orders or it was at your peril. No sympathy from the Sergeant Major. Reveille was going to be sounded at 0500hrs.

At least there were no parades or kit inspections the next day. He was giving us time to carry out some work on our kit.

The one thing we would have to do mid-morning the next day was an individual swimming assessment. I dreaded the thought of that, but it didn't stop me sleeping that night. The lights went out at ten o'clock and I think I must have been asleep by five past. I can't remember dreaming at all that night. Before I knew it, the whole world seemed to explode with the bugler playing Reveille, closely followed by Cpl Hutton making sure that we were awake with his own call of "hands off cocks and on socks!" You just had to get out of bed straight away, there was not even another five minutes. Most of us had not heard of the corporal's rally call, but I believe we all knew what it meant.

This was the start of twelve months of training, and getting to know those blokes you liked and those you didn't. When you bring forty young men together, all from different backgrounds, there will always be a certain amount of friction. I suppose like all groups of animals in this world, a pecking order was inevitable, but because we have developed brains it is easier for us to settle disputes and form comradeships, and we certainly settled down to become a unit.

We started to help each other with the cleaning of kit, and those who were in the know showed those who were learning. Now it was a question of putting in the time and energy rubbing down, spitting and polishing and general bull. Mind you, we were not going anywhere or doing anything else, so our full concentration could be given to our kit.

The boots took a long time, but they were always the pride and joy of any recruit. My parade boots were to last me all my military career. Ironing, pressing and starching were other activities that gave us a break from polishing.

It was during these sessions that you got to know more about others in the squad. There were some who had a lot to say and others who did the listening. One or two blokes had transferred from the Royal Navy or the Band Service, so they were older than most of us. I can't recall anyone being married, or at least admitting it. I certainly don't think a married person would be suited to the twelve-month training period.

But first the swimming assessment. First we had it explained to us what the eventual swimming test would consist of in week eleven at Deal. It was a test everyone had to pass. I couldn't believe what the PTI was telling us. Fully clothed in combat gear, with boots and rifle over the shoulder, you had to jump in and swim three lengths of the pool, then float for three minutes away from the sides. Then you had to get out of the pool, climb to the high board and jump off without killing yourself. The high board was VERY high.

In the meantime we were asked if anyone was a non-swimmer. Six of us raised our hands in acknowledgement of this failing. The Royal Marines have their own method of dealing with non-swimmers - two instructors, one each side of the pool, with very long poles. All six were invited to jump in at the deep end, and if they didn't want to jump a little assistance would be given. I say no more, but there was no health and safety in those days.

All sorts of different strokes were being attempted, the idea being to get to the other end, the motivation being the poles hovering just above your head. There would be no hesitation to push you either under or back to the middle if you tried to get to the side. Afterwards you were given the option of going to the pool for extra tuition in any free time you had. Eleven weeks is not a long time to develop enough skill to pass the test, but it was a must. I really hated swimming and had an aversion to water, maybe because at home in Leyton we only had a bath once a week. The official swimming periods in the training programme were two hours per week. I needed a lot more than that.

On the third day at Deal we got issued with our .303 rifles and bayonets. Just a few more items to clean and polish. Every weapon had a serial number, which it was our responsibility to remember. So now, here we were fully kitted and spurred and almost ready for drill and weapon training.

In the barrack room one or two of the boys were showing signs of home sickness and talking about leaving.

But on all the occasions when I was away from my family, I never felt homesick. I suppose it was because we never really had a home. Dear Mum did not have any input into our lives; she just was not alive long enough to teach us how to show love, affection and understanding. There were a number of occasions when I would have liked to have given Mum a call, asking for advice, but she was not there. Dad had too many distractions - the war, the evacuations, the loss of Mum, and trying to earn a living during the war. He had no input whatsoever as a parent. You can see why I was never homesick; I had to be a down-to-earth realist and a very calculated person.

Two lads eventually went 'over the wall', as it was called. One was brought back very quickly and suffered the due punishment. He was all right after that episode, he just needed to get it out of his system. We heard that the other lad, Recruit McMahon, went back across the water to Ireland and apparently joined another army. Those who tried to leave or thought about leaving were called mummy's boys, which was a bit cruel.

A lot of the other lads were loners and survivors, like myself, so it was a lot easier for us to cope with the hardships, the discipline and sometimes the loneliness within the mind. It could be called a hardness.

Going into week two of training, things started to get serious. It was becoming patently obvious that neither I, nor anyone else for that matter, was going to be allowed to play any representative sport, no matter how good we were. Priority was given to training. Training to become a smart, fit, disciplined Royal Marine initially and then on to become a Commando. It meant that soccer, cricket and all sports were put on the back burner for at least one whole year. Every minute of every hour was being taken up on a schedule that was planned and choreographed, based on the experience of training the elite over a long period of time.

From the moment that the bugle sounded for Reveille until lights out, we did not have a minute to squander or even to reflect on what else we could be doing. Perhaps when sitting together in the barrack room, in the evenings, whilst spit and polishing, thoughts could turn to Great Sampford village and the freedom that had been mine at that time. But there was no point in looking back, I was in it up to my neck. So it was a question of looking forward to achieving and succeeding, restrictions or no restrictions. The sport would come later, I hoped.

There were times when I considered that my tough childhood stood me in good stead. I had no desire to go back home, not like some of the other guys who had had a very happy family upbringing. They had things to miss and I could see that they had good reasons to be homesick. But already the bond and the strengthening of their characters allowed them in general to overcome their feelings of wanting to get home.

The comradeship in the barrack room was beginning to get a grip of every individual. There was the competition for who could get the shiniest toe caps and who could be the smartest on parade the next morning, and all the other little competitions that were going on, such as cleanest barrack room, best squad at drill and best recruit in the gym. All these challenges were there all the time.

The development of boy to man was becoming very apparent, and for people to say that all forms of competition in schools or anywhere is wrong, in my experience, breeds only weak characters. To say that competition makes individuals feel inferior is also wrong. It's not the competition, it's the fact that the individual is inferior - you will always have champions and losers. It's up to the losers to get stronger and better, otherwise they will always fall behind. Guts, will and determination will get your improvement. Only time will tell if I can make it.

Our instructors were expecting more and more from us and there were no excuses for getting things wrong. Barrack room inspection, if the room wasn't immaculate, would mean an extra inspection at night when we should have been spit-and-polishing our kit, so that was lost time which we had to make up for in our own time. Late on parade meant extra duties, such as spud bashing in the galley. Kit not up to standard on parade meant cleaning it again during lunch break and parading in front of the duty officer at night. Sloppy drill meant running around the parade ground with your rifle above your head in front of the whole parade or squad. Upsetting the sergeant major for any reason meant extra guard duties. The code of discipline was beginning to hit hard.

We all looked forward to weapon training instruction and range work, because it involved going up to

Kingsdown Ranges, and this meant a trip out in military transport, which gave us all a chance to see local people, from a distance of course. But it made you feel a little less isolated from the world outside.

Up at the ranges on top of the hill at Kingsdown, we would fire from 500 yards down to 100 yards at the targets in the butts. If we missed by miles the shots would go out to sea. Poor fishermen! In fact there was a danger zone out at sea which the fishermen recognised by the range flags that were flying.

At 11 o'clock precisely the NAAFI wagon would arrive at the ranges from the barracks. This period was called the 'stand easy' and we could buy hot tea and sticky buns. Of course in those days nearly everyone smoked, so there was time for a quick puff. That's if your fags weren't totally squashed or soaking wet. It was nice to see the ladies who carried out the NAAFI duties, even though they were motherly. They were brilliant because they were always there regardless of the weather conditions, a service very much appreciated by the lads.

It turned out that in the squad we had some first-class marksmen who were to go on to higher things in the shooting world later on in their careers. But in the meantime we all had to get to a very good standard.

After shooting and instruction was finished, we had to clean the barrels of our rifles with pull-throughs, "four by two" and hot water. You might wonder why, because the drill instructors on parade the next day would know that we had been on the range the day before, so they would pay special attention to the rifle inspection with the thumbnail test. And what is that, you might ask? It's a method whereby the right thumbnail is placed in the breech and the instructor looks down the barrel. With the light reflecting back from the thumbnail up the barrel, any dirt can be seen by the inspecting person. That was the theory.

In the third week of training it was considered that our kit was in good enough condition to have the squad photo taken. Mr Kidd, the local photographer, had the contract to take the photographs. This was very good business for him, because most of the squad would buy two copies each once they had seen the proofs. The process was a well-rehearsed routine, which all took place in the drill shed, we in our number two blues. Now we all felt part of the Royal Marines, because the photo would go into the archives and become part of the history of the Corps.

That evening, in a quiet moment, I tried to reflect how I was progressing. I felt that with the sessions in the gym, pull-ups, press-ups, running and the extra work in the swimming pool my fitness was getting better. But we weren't as yet doing anything up to commando level - that was still to come.

I was brought down to earth with a big bump, literally, one morning. We were fell in outside the Sergeant Major's office facing a brick wall. I was in the front rank on the edge of the kerb. I didn't know why, but for some reason I didn't feel very well, and we were stood to attention for some time. I knew that I was going to faint. The brick wall in front of me started to spin around. I was determined; I did not dare call out or move.

The next I knew was that I was coming round nose down on the pavement still at attention, but with different facial features. My nose was smashed, but little other damage had been done. The sick bay wasn't very far away, so I was soon taken care of by a medic. He cleaned me up, no stitches required, and asked me if I had had breakfast that morning. I told him I hadn't because I was on barrack-room cleaning duties. He advised me never to admit to not having had breakfast, or any meal, because it was a chargeable offence. I had learned a very valuable lesson.

So it was back to the squad on the parade for drill with a big plaster across my nose. I admit I was a bit embarrassed about the whole episode.

The next few weeks went along quite smoothly. The training went well and most of us had now settled into a routine. We were getting very good at doing the dhobi and ironing, polishing the floors with a big heavy buffer which had the technical name of 'bollicker'. I believe once you had any experience of using it you could see why it was called that.

Guard duties and galley duties were becoming less frequent, because we were no longer the junior squad. 651 squad had joined the previous week, so they were the new boys and we could march around with heads held high and chests out. We were beginning to look good on parade and our instructors could march us around with a bit of pride. If we looked good, it showed that they were doing their job properly.

The weeks were going by quite quickly now and soon

we would be going into the period of tests and pass-outs. But first it was the severe test of the kit muster, when every item of issued kit had to be marked with your name and laid out in accordance with the layout picture that had been on the barrack room wall since our arrival at Deal.

Shirts, socks, underwear and uniforms had to be folded in various shapes and sizes. Mess tins, eating irons, 'housewife' (needlework kit), cleaning brushes and bedding had to be folded precisely. Every single item had a reserved place and had to be immaculate. If your layout didn't please the Commanding Officer or the Adjutant, then you were always given a second chance at a very inconvenient time. Some instructors would tip the whole layout upside down and inside out so that it would take a lot of work to prepare for the re-inspection.

Week 10 meant the physical training test: pull up on the beams, rope climbing to the gym roof, touch and return to ground. There were press-ups, normally twenty or thereabouts, and circuit training with various activities at each post. This test was not too difficult, but it had to be passed to show that you were physically ready for the next stage of training, at Lympstone in Devon.

Week 11 was rehearsal week for the drill pass-out parade and the ultimate swimming test. I don't think anyone feared the pass-out parade, but there were a few racing hearts when it came to the swimming. Thursday morning was the actual test day, with Saturday being the retest for those who struggled.

I had put in a few hours of extra instruction in the pool

and was feeling fairly confident, but most certainly not overconfident. We were advised not to overdo the full English breakfast on the Thursday but to have a fair amount of porridge and carbohydrates in general.

We went down to the swimming baths at 0900hrs in our denim uniforms, carrying our swimming gear. Corporal Hutton marched us along, making sure our drill standard did not drop. At the baths, I felt very unsure about myself. That smell of cleansing fluid that all pools have didn't help one bit. I was very thankful old uniforms were supplied, which meant all our hard work on our kit wasn't washed away. Those who went first, the first six alphabetically, had a little bit of an advantage because the equipment was dry and therefore weighed less. I was to be in the second group.

We sat out on the side to cheer the others on, as required. It looked as though the first six were good swimmers. They appeared to have no problem with the two lengths, fully clothed with boots, weapon webbing and tin helmet. Most individuals used the breast stroke to conserve energy, though there was one good swimmer who used the crawl. Then it was the three minutes of floating on your back or face without touching the sides. The more confident you were, the more towards the middle of the pool you stayed. They all got through that part. Then out of the water, straight to the diving boards and up to the top of, I believe, the five-metre board. No hesitation, jump straight off, making sure that your tin helmet was very secure. One lad hesitated for some time before being persuaded to jump.

The first six got out of their kit and I got dressed in cold wet clothing. I told myself to jump in and swim, and did so.

A breast stroke of sorts got me there and back, and now came the bit I dreaded, the float. I had been advised by one of the swimming instructors to try and relax and keep plenty of air in the lungs, which would help to keep me floating. Breathing out too often meant you would start to sink.

I tried not to panic but at one point I got a mouthful of water, which I didn't like. Choking and spluttering, I started to use my arms, then I remembered that this was frowned upon so I stopped. Three minutes seemed like an eternity, so I took a very big breath and hoped that I could last out. I was close to giving up when I remembered my promise to myself on the train journey down. Give one hundred per cent and be sure in the knowledge that they would not let you drown. Yes, yes, yes! The whistle went - I had done it.

The adrenalin was still rushing as I got to the top of the board and walked straight off the end. I had forgotten to tighten the chin strap, and as I hit the water the tin helmet hit the rifle, which then hit me round the ears. I tried not to show any pain, only joy.

We took a shower and watched the others go through their paces. It was the longest five minutes of my life so far. Everybody made it, without having to go back on the Saturday. One week to go.

We had a weapon training and handling test and then

the pass-out parade. Although we had been at Deal for almost three months, we were not allowed to explore the barracks and were very restricted to certain areas. It was only later on in my career that I learned of the wonderful sporting facilities in the barracks.

As a squad we had progressed very well, and there were very few punch-ups in the barrack room. Corporal Hutton took great care in pinching out that sort of thing in the bud and as individuals we were so busy in the evenings that explosions with clashes of character just didn't seem to develop. We blended into a very good squad.

The next period of training at Lympstone looked like testing the team spirit a bit more. We were told that it would be more of an individual effort, every man for himself to ensure that you went forward to carry out commando training at Bickleigh.

But that's looking a bit too far ahead. We still had one more week at Deal. Time to make a concerted effort on our uniforms and boots for the final parade. Sergeant Tyack had us drilling and more drilling with the full Royal Marine Deal Band to ensure that it was going to be right on the day. He and Cpl Hutton were going were going to escort us to Lympstone to ensure that no one did a runner and that the freedom of the journey did not go to our heads. Apparently our kit was going by road in military vehicles and would arrive pretty much at the same time as our train from London.

The last couple of days at Deal, Thursday and Friday, went very quickly indeed. The pass-out parade in front of the commanding officer went well, with the band in full ceremonial and 650 squad marching to the regimental march, *A Life On The Ocean Wave*. It was a parade to remember with great pride. The next day was for returning all items of weaponry that belonged to the armoury at Deal

We had to pack our personal items of kit and clothing carefully in our kitbags, which were to be loaded onto the vehicles in the MT yard where they would be guarded overnight. We were left with the suitcases we had joined with for travel items needed en route to Lympstone.

A little celebration was allowed in the NAAFI that night with all the staff who had got us through the last twelve weeks. It was a chance for us to say thank you. A good night's sleep was a must before the journey.

I woke up before reveille, probably because of the excitement. I was anticipating a few hours out of the barracks, a great rail trip first to London, then down to Topsham station, between Exeter and Exmouth. I had a good wash and shave early so that all my personal items could be stowed away.

The eating irons would have to wait, because a good breakfast was high on my priority list for that morning.

The train was due to leave Deal station at 1000hrs. We had to fall in outside the company office at 0900hrs and there was no way I was going to faint this time. The sergeant major would no doubt have a few words of advice to give us all before we were marched out of the barracks.

As we were paraded outside the office, we saw the two three-ton trucks with our kit on board leave the yard. We knew then that the next phase of our training, a more physical phase, was almost upon us. It was just that point that the sergeant major emphasised, among his farewell comments. He wished us all good luck. Sergeant Tyack turned us to the right and quick marched us to a new adventure.

CHAPTER FIVE

—◆—

The steam journey to London was brilliant. The squad had a complete carriage to itself, which made it a lot easier for our instructors to keep tabs on us all. There was no need for any of us to go to the refreshment carriage because we all had been issued with a bag ration, with a drink. Mind you it would have felt more realistic (and rather amazing) to have sat among the people of the world who were doing their daily thing, and even maybe got involved in a conversation. I could imagine that most of the questions would have been one way. "Where are you going lads, what are you doing"? But it was not to be.

At midday we arrived at Waterloo Station, where we had to get across from Platform 3 to Platform 5. We had loads of time, because the West Country train wasn't leaving until 1400hrs. The train was parked on Platform 5, so we could board it without delay and get comfortable. The same arrangements had been made with Western Rail, so we had our own carriage. That was a shame really, because the lads would have loved to investigate the rest of the train, for all sorts of reasons.

It was obvious that the military were very experienced at these sorts of moves, but there is always at least one person who can't be found. Now it was getting close to departure time and it was Taff Price who was missing. He was found in the heads (toilets) in the next carriage, having gone there because ours was occupied. He said he couldn't wait, so he had used the one next door. I understood that in those days you couldn't use the loo while the train was in the station. Try telling that to Recruit Price.

Those of us who still had some sarnies left settled down to a lunch session while the train was still stationary. At 1400hrs precisely the train started to pull out of the station, but by then most of the boys were asleep. The clickety-click of the wheels on the track was a great background to the sound of snoring and grunting. I was soon to join them. Come 1600hrs, the train was pulling into Exeter Station, and that was when most of us woke up. Those who didn't were soon encouraged to do so by Corporal Hutton. Part of this train was going on down to Plymouth and Cornwall, while our part plus one other carriage was staying with this engine and going on to Exmouth. The carriages which were disconnected from ours were soon reconnected to another engine. We were then on our way for the last leg of our journey. It was only about thirty minutes before we arrived at Topsham Station, where there was a Royal Navy coach and a minibus waiting for us.

The camp was only five minutes' drive from the station. The main entrance was quite impressive, with a member of the provost staff in full blues manning the main gate.

The vehicles stopped at the guardroom and Sergeant

Tyack got out to report to the Guard Commander and to find out where our accommodation block was. A member of the guard escorted the vehicles to our block. Our new room Corporal, Corporal Jackson, was waiting to usher us into the block and to issue us our individual bed spaces. The bedding was already at the head of the bed and our kitbags were at the foot of the bed, so the bed spaces had been allocated on our behalf. No arguing there.

Looking out of the window, we could all see that this was a very different camp and a very different proposition from Deal. At the bottom of the camp was a railway line, in fact the one that we had just come in on, and on the other side of the line was the River Exe. Backing on to the railway line was the Tarzan course and rope climbs, which seemed to go up to the clouds. The whole setup was in a large field next to the gymnasium, which was known as Stalag 15. I wonder why.

We were to find out, because we were going to spend a lot of time and effort in that particular area. It looked awesome and frightening.

The introduction at Lympstone was very similar to that at Deal. There was an introduction to our instructors, only there were more of them. It was a good time of the year to be at Lympstone, because most of our training was going to be outside, on the Tarzan course, the Woodbury cross country course and on the roads and parade ground. In this camp the weather stopped nothing. Some time would be spent in the gym and on the rifle ranges.

In the meantime we had to sort out our kit and neatly

stow it away. We now had approximately fifteen weeks of extreme physical training and one week as the King Squad, for those who made it. Our bodies were going to be punished and bruised. It was very important for us as individuals to make sure we had as many pairs of good socks as we could afford to buy and to make sure our combat boots were well worn in, because of all the mileage that was going to be done in them.

The first week was a build-up of practice around the Tarzan course, with the fireman's lift and run and the rope climb. The PTIs started off by giving us a programme of exercises to match faces to ability. Everything physical from now on was aimed at the tests in weeks fourteen and fifteen, all of which had to be done in a time frame. We were given in writing a weekly programme of events in two-hourly periods, two periods in the morning and two in the afternoon.

Sometimes in the morning we would start the day's activities with a run around the Tarzan course, followed by a fifty-yard fireman's run and then a march/run of about three miles to Woodbury Common, where we would receive map-reading instruction and practice. Then there was a march/run back to camp for lunch.

The pace each day was increased and the tempo was rising. The expectation of our bodies was increasing and so the expectations of the instructors kept rising.

Two of the squad, Taylor and Edwards, sustained badly-damaged knee joints, caused by falling from the bridge across the Tarzan course. They were given ten days to get repaired medically and back into the squad. The one thing nobody wanted was to get back-squadded. This was every young man's nightmare scenario, because the next squad hadn't left Deal yet and therefore a couple more weeks would be lost. In the meantime our squad would be getting fitter and stronger. Any lost time would be difficult to make up.

The programme often changed. On occasion we would start the day with a run/march to Woodbury, across the cross-country course and through the sheep dip tunnel and then a run/march back to camp, the time being noted. Now we were soaking wet and the rope climb came next, with an aim of two minutes. The Tarzan course had its own time limit of 4 minutes 55 seconds, but as yet we were not expected to get close to that.

Good news - after seven days Taylor and Edwards came back to us. They would be very carefully watched for the next three days to make sure they had recovered enough to continue with the squad. The Company Commander and Sergeant Major would hopefully give them the good news. In the event they both made it.

I must admit that I personally was beginning to feel the pace a bit. But I think the farm work had helped my upper body development, and from that point of view I was coping well. From the cardio aspect I seemed to be able to manage the distances, but carrying backpacks and very wet clothing all the time was taking a toll on my legs. This weakness tended to play on my mind, and I found it difficult to keep up with the rest of them when running in ranks. The temptation was to drop back, and that was fatal as far as the instructors were concerned. Names went into mental notebooks to be discussed at the instructors' meetings when making assessments of individuals. When running on your own against the clock, you can adjust your pace according to conditions and your own feelings. Let's remember that the nine-mile and 30-mile speed marches were in file formation. I would have to work on my leg strengthening.

When I felt low, it would have been good to be able to contact the family and talk it over. But for me that was out of the question. I would have liked to have a chat with brother Jim, but this was the 1950s - no mobile phones, in fact very few phones of any kind. So it would have had to be a letter to Jim, and I didn't know where he was. You had to sort yourself out alone.

I spoke to one of the young PTI corporals about strengthening my legs. He said that I could do leg exercises in the barrack room, sitting on a hard chair with legs together and a weight of some form tied to the feet. Then you swing the lower part of the leg from the knee down backwards and forwards, about thirty repetitions at a time.

It was half way through our training at Lympstone, and things generally were going very well. In week 10 we would, if performing well, get our first shore leave into Exmouth. A dance apparently was laid on at the Palace. So that was something to look forward to. But first there was a lot of work to be done in final preparation for the tests. The momentum was building and most of the lads were feeling quite optimistic about getting to the end.

The rope climb, which was very high, required a pull-up with the arms, followed by a push-up with the legs, once you had gripped the rope between crossed boots. Depending when the PTIs fitted this exercise into the routine, it could become more difficult. If it followed the fireman's lift, your legs were still shaking from the carry, so your luck was out if the bloke you had to carry on the lift was huge. Hard luck son!

In between all this physical there were a number of periods on the parade ground keeping the squad's drill level up to scratch. There were guard duties, patrols around the camp, ceremonial guards sometimes, then it was best blues and sentry duty at key points. If you were near the main gate and the parade ground/officers' mess, you had to be very alert and continually coming to attention to give the appropriate salute. The patrols around the camp were much preferred by us recruits because they were more relaxed.

Friday next, all being well, was shore leave night. Best blues were the dress of the day. There was an inspection by the Guard Commander or the duty officer. Handkerchiefs were a must, along with temporary leave passes and knowledge on how to behave and what time leave finished. Quite often one was sent back to the barrack room to get a handkerchief or an answer to a question.

Being allowed out of the camp on your own for the first time since joining the Royal Marines was definitely something to look forward to. The best idea was to go out in small groups of about three or four mates.

Before that, we had a very tough day ahead of us. It was the nine-miler, one hour of pain and trouble, starting and finishing at the main gate. Having gone in a large half circle via Woodbury, part of the course would be very familiar. If you turned right out of the gate you started off on the flat and finished coming up the hill from Exeter direction, which was more difficult. So our destiny was in the hands of the senior PTI and his frame of mind that morning. We had to hope his missus had been kind to him the night before and that they hadn't had an argument.

So was it going to be right or left at the gate? We would only know at 1000hrs tomorrow.

That evening all the lads seemed to be in a jovial mood, probably because most of them believed that tomorrow would be a relatively easy day. After the nine miler and lunch, all we had was two hours of drill.

That evening, while we were laughing and joking, Chalky White came up with a cracker. Someone had told him that that on the night of the shore leave the local queer (gay) old boy from Woodbury village would tour up and down the Exmouth road in his open sports car, offering lifts to the boys, mainly on their way back late at night. "I'll be looking for him" said Chalky, all six foot three and 14 stone of him. I don't know where he got the information from, but it made us laugh and made us aware of him.

It also triggered a discussion in the room about it. Would any one of us, or anyone in the forces generally, dare to admit to being gay or to show any signs of it? The general consensus was that at that time in the fifties, it just would not happen. It was inconceivable that anyone would join the forces knowing they were gay. It would have been deeply frowned upon, and almost certainly the person would have been drummed out of the service for contaminating the minds and morals of our young men – if you weren't you would have been ridiculed out by the young men themselves. It was felt, although not mentioned in the same words, that political correctness would not have ridden roughshod over the discipline and common sense of the military. At that time it was felt by the lads in the room that there was no way that 'coming out' or admitting you were gay was an option. There were just no signs, certainly in the Royal Marines, that the problem existed. The discussion went on for some time and in the end it was felt that this subject should be added to the other taboo subjects.

You did not talk about politics and religion because the atmosphere always got overheated and led to trouble. Discipline was much more important. As far as I remember the subject was never mentioned again, even in jest. It certainly didn't stay on the mind for very long.

We needed a good night's sleep before the nine-miler. On waking up, it was a big "Oh no!" It was pouring with rain. Would it keep going all morning? We washed, shaved and went across for breakfast, a hearty one I might add.

Everyone seemed very chatty, a question of nerves maybe. Come 0930hrs the order was given to fall in, and it was still raining a little. We had to march, rifles across our shoulders, from the company office to the main gate, where we were joined by six PTIs. "Break into double time" was the order, and we were followed by the safety vehicle and medical team. Through the main gate and the order given was left turn. Yes! Thank you Mrs PTI, maybe they felt sympathetic towards us because of the weather. No, Royal Marine senior ranks don't think like that.

Anyway we were not moaning - we were on our way. All went well until we had done about five miles, when Ginger Grant started to fall behind. The lads wanted to drop back with him to give him a hand, but the PTIs said that he was their problem and responsibility, so we had to continue. I was feeling the pace a bit, and it was just at that point that Gubby fell out of the ranks. The medics had a good look at him and put him in to the back of the truck. In the meantime Ginger was still going, albeit at his own pace.

Before long we were turning down Woodbury Lane, so we knew it was not far to the barracks. That boosted us, and we finished with a flourish and marched through the main gates with heads held high. Poor Gubby would have to do it again.

A shower, nice hot cup of tea, lunch and soon we were ready for the drill session. There were a few very stiff drill movements that afternoon, but we got through it without upsetting the parade staff too much. It was good to see that no one had to run round the parade ground with rifle above head.

The shore leave went very well. Six of us went together. We got out of the main gate with no penalties and caught the bus directly outside.

We had a drink in the Bell and on to the dance. It was packed with locals and most of our squad, but it seemed that most of my group of lads didn't care too much about dancing. It was great to relax, have a drink and a laugh and generally view the talent. There was very little point in getting involved with the girls because we would be gone in a few weeks, three to be precise.

The last bus was due to go back to the barracks area at 2230hrs and we agreed to catch it rather than walk. That's what we did, and we passed the Guard Commander's wary eye as we handed in our leave passes.

The following morning there were some hilarious stories about how the shore leave had gone. Dusty Miller boasted that he had struck lucky with a chambermaid from the hotel just down the road from the dance. He said she was no teenager and it seemed it was a routine of hers to trap young marines at this particular dance. She had invited him back to her staff room at the hotel. He thought she had gone for him because he was on his own. They left the dance very early, he said, otherwise he would never have got back to the barracks before 2359hrs, the deadline. He said it was a great night, without going into many details, and well worth the taxi fare which got him back on time.

One or two of the lads said they had met some very nice young ladies. There were some nurses from Exeter hospital who apparently had an invitation every time a new squad got their shore leave. I can't recall that anyone mentioned meeting Sports Car Bill from Woodbury, but then I don't suppose they would have talked about it if they had.

The next week was full of personal tests, probably the severest physical demands so far and a must to pass to go forward to commando training at Bickleigh camp. It seems as though I am forever talking about the physical side of this training, but I can assure you that that was exactly how life was on a day-to-day basis. It was noticeable that our fitness levels had risen to the point where coping with the demands had become less stressful.

One of the very good attitudes at Lympstone was that the fatigue duties, which were like those at Deal, potato bashing, pot-washing and office cleaning, were kept to a bare minimum, because it was considered more beneficial to devote one's time and effort to getting fit. We certainly appreciated that attitude. But a very high level of discipline was still maintained throughout the time at Lympstone.

So to weeks 11 and 12 and a final effort to pass the Tarzan course, the fireman's run, the rope climb, the cross-country map run and the 30-miler. Would we make it or have to retake it? Only time would tell. Events were coming along so fast and furious that it was a physical blur. It was difficult to switch off and stop worrying about it all, because failure now would be just unbearable.

For this squad the sequence of events was going to be critical, so I suggested to a couple of the lads that we should find time to go to the barracks cinema and see a couple of films, just to relax a bit - to me it didn't really matter what the films were. Was the pressure getting to me, just me? I was hoping others would agree to the film idea. They did, and about half a dozen of us managed to fit into the cinema on the Saturday evening, which broke the weekend up for us. It was a Western and a Tom and Jerry.

The following week was a mixture of parade work, weapon training and gym work, culminating on the Thursday and Friday with the physical pass-out tests.

I am going to explain this part from a personal point of view. The cross-country and sheep dip were followed by the Tarzan course. The time allowed was one hour from leaving the gate to completing the final part of the Tarzan course, which was the wall climb and jump. This was very much an individual thing, and we were watched all the way by PTIs at checkpoints.

I got back to camp in 52 minutes after Woodbury, of course soaking wet. This gave me eight minutes to complete the Tarzan course. I went straight into it and was going fairly well when I fell off the rope bridge into the mud and had to go back to cover the rope bridge again. My legs were hurting something awful. The crawl through the rope net took its toll with a touch of cramp and that hurt, but I couldn't stop. I had a 50-yard run to the finish. The instructor shouted at me that I had just two minutes to get over the wall. The cramp was tightening up. The wall was eight feet high, which required a jump and pull up and over with a prop on the other side. I missed my run and pull up the first time and had to use up valuable time for the second attempt. This time I got it, pull up and over.

I was tired and the cramped leg was painful. I only had 30 seconds left to spare, so it was close.

Now a short break before the fireman's lift and rope climb. We had two minutes to complete the 100 yards lift and run, and I was lucky I had little Jeff Benstead to carry, then he had me. We made it, so now it was up the rope. I was a little worried about the cramp, so I tried to use my arms more than normal. It was tough, but with no time limit you could pace it better. I tell you I came down a lot faster than I went up.

We who had finished waited to cheer the others as they ran and staggered down from the main gate. It was good to see both Ginger Grant and Gubby were within the time allowed as they passed on to the Tarzan course. Great encouragement was given to them. In thirty minutes the whole thing would be over.

After lunch, in clean clothes and rested, we were to parade in the gymnasium and the morning's timings were given. My fingers were crossed that a re-run would not be required, as at that moment I could not contemplate it. There were three over-time failures who would run again tomorrow. It was a relief to me that I was not one of them, although I did feel very sorry for those lads.

The next day was going to be a personal maintenance day, known as a 'make and mend', washing and cleaning all the kit that was filthy from the last two days' efforts.

Those unlucky three were going to be re-tested. Good luck lads. We got permission to encourage them over the last phase in the camp. They all made it, well done.

So we had just the 30-miler and then it was all downhill with drill and parade work as the King's squad.

A kind of sword of honour called 'King's Badgeman' would be nominated at the end of the final week. We had good ideas who we thought would be the recipient, but our ideas were sometimes different from those of the senior instructors.

We had just two days to prepare ourselves for the 30-miler. Apparently we would get taken out to the edge of Dartmoor near Okehampton and then work our way back to Lympstone. We hoped it wouldn't be pouring with rain. Thirty miles is a long way even when you're dry, so we didn't want soggy socks, boots and clothing.

Friday was upon us very quickly and it was time for the big one. We had a bag ration given to us at breakfast, and made sure that our water bottles were full. The half bottle of navy rum was in the left pouch (only joking). By three o'clock in the afternoon it would all be over, but first it was into the back of the three-tonner and away.

Some mornings you feel really bright and perky, but on this particular one I felt rough and sluggish. I hoped that I wasn't going down with something nasty like flu or a gastric problem. No, this day had to be right. Pull yourself together, I kept telling myself, but the truck journey wasn't helping at all.

The lead in this task was taken by Lieutenant Steve Jones, I suppose to set an example and show it could be done. Every six miles we would stop and have a drink and a short break. Once again the safety vehicle was behind us, and we had two of the squad fifty yards in front and two lads fifty yards behind as a warning to other road users.

After every stop these four lads would be changed. I was hoping to get a chance at those duties, because it gave you other things to think of rather than your aches and pains.

The first two six-mile sessions went all right for me personally, but I was still feeling a bit rough. Twelve to eighteen miles on I really started to fall behind and I felt sick. I kept going, just, but after a further four miles I pulled over and was very sick in the ditch. One instructor stopped with me for a while and after a drink of water I felt a lot better. I don't know if it was something I'd had in the NAAFI the previous night that had upset me, but I recovered and the instructor corporal paced me back to the squad just in time for the next six-mile break.

As luck would have it I was then selected to be one of the up front markers with Ginger Grant. At that time I wasn't sure if I should eat my bag ration, but I decided to have just the chocolate bar to replace some of the sugar lost.

It was great being out front as traffic guide and marker, because you could go at your own stride and your mind was taken off your fatigue. Looking back at the boys in three ranks, it appeared that a number of them were flagging, and a constant watch was being kept by the instructors, just to make sure that nobody was in serious trouble. Before long we were coming to the outskirts of Exeter and ready for the next and last six-mile break. Just one session left to get to the barracks. Surely we could make it now.

I was back in the ranks with the others and with

renewed vigour. As we got closer to Lympstone you could see and feel the pride in the lads, and the tempo of the pace was increased slightly. Going up the last hill to the barracks, Officer Commanding Steve Jones stopped us for a minute or two to allow the stragglers to catch up and so that we all could adjust our uniforms and headgear so as to march through the main gates as a complete unit. We did it with heads held high at a smart pace. "Well done everybody" were the last words from the OC before we were dismissed. There was a big cheer from us all as we entered our barrack block, followed by a big rush for the showers and baths. A lot of time was spent in each.

Now came a week of ceremonial duties on the parade ground. Before that though, the Sergeant Major had us all assembled in the lecture room to brief us on the procedure for our move, to Bickleigh camp on Monday week.

Once again our kit was to be packed into our kitbags on the Sunday night, leaving only the combat dress for travelling on the Monday with our large backpacks. We immediately sensed something different. Our luggage would be transported by road to Bickleigh, leaving us with overnight personal belongings, which would be carried in our backpacks with a spare set of clothing. We would be transported to the centre of Dartmoor, where we would be put into groups of three, with compass and map. Then we were to find our way across the moor to Bickleigh Camp, where 42 Commando and the Commando Training Centre were based. On arrival we would report to the CTC Sergeant Major, who would accommodate us. The earlier we arrived the more choice of the better Nissen huts we would have. There were nine ranks to a Nissen hut.

There was nothing luxurious at Bickleigh, we were told. "You will know when you've arrived because you have to climb up Heartbreak Hill and you'll know that when you see it", the Sergeant Major smiled. "Don't get lost, Dartmoor is not a good place to spend a night lost. Good luck!"

I felt I would be all right because my great-grandmother five times removed on my mother's side had been a member of the Baskerville family, Catherine Baskerville. She married my ancestor Thomas Anthony in 1795, so she would have the people out there on the Moor and the Hounds of course to take care of my group!

We think the Sergeant Major told us the details so early so that we could study the maps in detail to make sure we knew what route to take when the time came. We could, if crafty, find a lot of the route by road, but we didn't know what the groups were going to be and who was travelling with who, and we didn't know the start point either. So everyone would have to study the map. But it was a help knowing in advance.

The last week started quietly brushing up on our drill, and as the week went by the drill became more a rehearsal for the final pass-out parade. Families had been told it was taking place on the Saturday and were given the chance to visit the barracks and witness it.

I don't know if anyone in my family was interested enough to come down to Devon. I certainly did not expect them to, and I would have been very surprised if they had turned up. I don't think too many of the squad had any idea who was going to come. I thought the distance and finding accommodation would be a problem for most.

Priority was given in the evening to cleaning our best blues and white webbing, which we were determined to get to the very highest of standards. To get picked up on your pass-out parade for lack of standard would not go down very well with anybody. We hoped the sun was going to shine for the final episode of our training at Lympstone. We knew best blues would not be dress of the day very often at Bickleigh. We were told on a number of occasions by many different people that it was going to be tough. We expected it to be so, and the daily dress code would reflect it accordingly.

A couple of our instructors, the junior ones in particular, had told us in the quieter moments just what was at Bickleigh: the rope crossing at the Vale, a regain halfway across the river. Then a death slide through the trees, in all 125 yards long from approximately 60 yards up in the sky to ground level. Then Bickleigh Tor, which was about a thousand feet high. It was all part of the daily fitness routine. Unarmed combat was going to be an interesting part of the training, but the climb up Heartbreak Hill every time you were going back to camp would put a bit of fear in our hearts.

We had now been training for about 32 weeks, with about twelve or thirteen weeks to go. At the end of this would be the coveted Green Beret and then Christmas leave, prior to posting. That was the plan, but circumstances were to change all that.

Final parade day turned out to be pretty good, weatherwise. The parade time was to be 1100hrs and we had to fall in outside the block at 1030 and march 100 yards on to the parade ground. The CO had invited the Major General to take the parade. The Plymouth Band, in full regalia, were present to march us onto the parade ground. We were required to give a demonstration of our drill and marching skills before carrying out the march past, with the MGRM taking the salute. He would then address us and present the King's Badge to those who had earned it. After being dismissed we could mingle with our families in the NAAFI canteen for tea and cakes.

About fifteen of the squad families came to the parade, and there were about forty family members there all together. We now had a lovely quiet weekend to look forward to with a bit of relaxation, and maybe even a beer over in the NAAFI. I felt so very proud of myself for getting as far as this stage. But the Green Beret was the ultimate, so there was still a lot of work to do to achieve that. I had to keep my concentration and energy levels as high as possible. But at that moment I could almost have switched off.

I went to bed fairly early and intended to go to the Barrack Church service in the morning after breakfast to give thanks for being kept safe so far. The rest of the day could be used in packing my kit for transit. We also had to hand in our rifles and bayonets to the armoury.

CHAPTER SIX

The last stage of this very long journey was about to begin. *Mum, why aren't you here to see all this?* I thought. *I hope that wherever you are you can get a glimpse of what is going on.*

On Monday morning in the back of a three-ton truck we said farewell to Lympstone and put our faith into the hands of the Commando Training Centre, Bickleigh, courtesy of 42 Cdo RM. We arrived at a spot on Dartmoor given by a grid reference and the names of the groups of three were read out. At 1100hrs the first group was dropped off at the first grid, then the second group was dropped at the next grid about half a mile away and so on until all the groups had been dispatched.

First it was a question of finding where you were on the map. I was with Dusty Miller and Alan Murphy and we decided to take off in the known direction and then decide on the route to take and mark it on the map and stick to that route to the end. Dusty Miller read the compass and Murphy and I took it in turns to read the map and follow the route. We had checkpoints marked on the map which were highlighted and Dusty was responsible for getting us to the next checkpoint. It was quite a relaxing jaunt, because there was no real pressure or time factor. It appeared that we had approximately fifteen miles to travel, which meant that we should arrive at about 1500hrs at the latest.

There was a very direct route across Dartmoor towards Two Bridges and a slightly more circular route towards Tavistock. The Two Bridges route was shorter but over very rough terrain and difficult to map-read. We had previously marked the northern route and were coming into Bickleigh via the flatter part of Dartmoor edge, so on this occasion we would miss Heartbreak Hill. At this stage we were all feeling pretty hearty, so we ate our bag ration on the hoof and didn't stop for a pub beer. No pubs!

At 1400hrs we were approaching Bickleigh Vale road in good spirits, but looming over to our left we could see very dark and threatening rain clouds just above the Two Tors. Spud Murphy suggested that we should catch a Dartmoor pony each and ride the rest of the way. It would look great going through the main gate on ponies shouting "The cavalry's arrived!" We had a good laugh visualising catching a pony, let alone riding one. We decided to go by shanks' pony at the double. We felt pretty strong and didn't want to get a soaking. It was just as well, because as we got to the camp barrier it started tipping down. The sentry saw us coming and waved us through and told us where to go.

This was really an old wartime camp made up of Nissen huts. The Sergeant Major ticked us off the nominal role and told us to go to hut 79, where our kit had already been stowed. So much for hut selection. There were three other lads already there and they had got the central fire going. They had come from the direct route, where it had been raining for some time, so they were drying out their clothes.

We three decided to scout the camp to find out where all the important facilities were. The galley looked very antiquated, but there was a NAAFI of sorts, so we had tea and buns. The CTC office block was three Nissen huts together. We went to check company orders to see if our routine for tomorrow had been posted - It hadn't, so we bravely asked the Sergeant Major what the routine was going to be, and he told us to get settled in and briefed. So it was back to Hut 79 to get ourselves sorted out.

We still had large kit lockers and standard beds. The heads were at the end of the hut, sort of en suite. The showers and washing room were in a different hut fifty yards away and winter was coming. The fire was going to get a lot of use. Maybe now while it was quiet we should find out where the coal and wood supply was, so we could stock up in readiness. Next to the fire was a coal bunker, but there wasn't much coal in it. It was worth finding out where the supply came from, so Dusty and I went scavenging. The quartermaster's compound was over to the left of the camp, so that's where we headed.

The QM storeman told us it was a do-it-yourself task. "You get the sacks from just over there" he said, pointing vaguely to the right. Over we went, and filled a couple of sacks to start with. Luckily there was a wheelbarrow, so it wasn't too bad getting the load back to Hut 79. We suggested to the other lads that if we all went over we could stock up with plenty of coal and wood. They agreed it was a good idea to do it before the guys in the other huts twigged. So we got the jump and had a good stock.

With all gear stowed away, bed made, it was time for a nap. The next thing I knew there was lots of shouting and shaking. We had to fall in outside the company office in fifteen minutes, so across we went. It appeared by the number of ranks that the whole squad had arrived.

The Sergeant Major fell us in and marched us to what we now knew as the cinema for a briefing and introduction to the commando training staff. He said that over the last eight months of training, we had progressively been involved in more and more demanding and potentially character-building tasks and challenges, culminating in the very testing methods now employed here at Bickleigh Camp. He questioned why should we doubt that any of the very dangerous things that we were expected to carry out could possibly go wrong. Why should there be any real danger? These tests had been carried out in this way for a long period of time. He didn't tell us about any accidents, and anyway, if there had been any, after all they were only accidents.

Looking back, there were no health and safety barriers. There were also no safety nets or harnesses. If you fell off the river crossing rope, then you fell 20ft into the river and you had to get back on to the rope to perform the regain. On the Death Slide you made sure that you got a very good grip of the rope, because if you fell you most certainly would be dead. Hence the name. He said that all the facilities for training were outside the camp at Bickleigh Tor, the Vale and Dartmoor, which of course meant that there was a lot of hoofing to be done every day. He also said that commando training was going to be even more physical than we had experienced so far, but barring injury there should be no reason why we would not succeed, having got to this stage. He appeared very confident that his staff would get us through. From our point of view, that was good news, or was he just having us on?

This was a new phase of training, cliff climbing, abseiling and grenade practice, sprinkled with a little unarmed combat. From next Monday morning training would commence in earnest.

Monday morning started with a visit from Plymouth CID, to give us a lecture on drugs and for us to experience the different smells related to them. The lecture was not so much to warn us off the use of them but to help us recognise anyone using them. It was a brilliant lecture and demo in as much as it was unique. It was a subject that in the military in the 1950s we were very unlikely to come across. The self-discipline instilled in all Royal Marines was the barrier to drugs and other illegal stimulants. I think self-belief is stronger than any need to use drugs.

In that first week of training at Bickleigh we had a day testing gas masks, which involved going into a gas chamber with a mask on. I don't know to this day exactly what gas was used, but once inside we had to run on the spot to make sure that even with very heavy breathing no gas got inside. The instructor told us to hold our breath and remove the mask, then replace the gas mask in the dark. The aim was to get it back on before you ran out of breath. If you didn't it was a mad rush to the door to get outside. At this stage one or two came out gasping and coughing, so I'm sure the gas was not too toxic or dangerous. In a real war scenario I wouldn't fancy an experience with gas.

This camp really could be classed as hardship living area, though it was not so bad for us as we were only there for a short time. Apparently way over on the far side where 42 Commando were housed, a big building project was under way to modernise all the accommodation blocks, because the camp was going to be the permanent residence of the Commandos. So a lot of work was required to get it up to any standard at all.

Almost every day we would have a run down the big hill and either tackle Bickleigh Tor or the river crossing and death slide, sometimes both, before coming back up the hill. But first, it was grenade training at special ranges at the back of the camp. It turned out to be a lot of fun, even though it was a very serious training session. First of all, using dummy grenades, we had to go through the routine of withdrawing the pin, making sure that you held on to the lever, then an overarm throw, then get down very low and wait for the explosion. If there was no explosion, then hazard drill had to be carried out to ensure full safety. All this took place behind a concrete barrier, for obvious reasons. Once the instructor was happy with your practice routine he would say to you "This one is for real, please make sure you do not drop it!" There was a wry smile on his face, but it all had to be taken very seriously.

If a grenade was dropped, there was a second concrete barrier just a foot or so away and close enough to get behind. The grenades had been primed with long fuses on purpose as a safety factor. When it was my turn, I had a funny feeling of power as I threw the grenade. Taking the pin out reminded me of war films I had seen.

After the serious business was complete the instructors had arranged a target-throwing competition whereby the throw nearest to a supposed German machine gun position about fifty yards away would win the recruit a free meal in the NAAFI with a beer. I was hoping that my cricketing days would help me get close to the target, but no such luck. The honour went to Jeff Benstead.

Then we were off to Sennybridge for two days of cliff climbing and abseiling. There was a temporary camp there to sleep us overnight. We had two 24-hour ration packs each to self-feed. This approach to feeding was new to us, but would become very familiar to us all in our future careers.

Three three-ton trucks arrived outside the CTC office as we mustered at 0900hrs straight after breakfast. Full combat gear was the dress of the day. It wasn't a long journey, but once again it was great to get out and about. The OC and medical team followed in the Land Rover, so it was quite a convoy. It was raining very hard when we left and one of the instructors made a comment that this was not good for cliff climbing.

Luck was with us, because the weather improved as we went along, and by the time that we arrived at Sennybridge it was a lovely sunny morning. Each truck carried a lot of rope.

I wasn't sure how I was going to cope with the heights involved in cliff climbing and abseiling. The jump off the top board at Deal was high, but nothing like as high as this was going to be. This experience was going to be totally different. I sincerely hoped I didn't freeze and make a fool of myself. The instruction would be top notch and the technique would be sound and well proven.

The climb really wasn't a problem. Although you weren't attached to anything, there was a rope hanging from above and as long as you didn't lose you grip you were pretty safe. I enjoyed that part. What I found much more difficult and frightening was going over the cliff on a run down. This time you had a rope belt around your waist and the main run down rope was attached to your rope belt, through a loop which was doubled back on itself. So it became a brake as you pulled back on it.

The really scary bit was walking over the edge of the cliff face down and having to rely totally on the rope to take your weight, once you were over the cliff edge. It was almost like (I would imagine) committing suicide. Your weight then set you in motion and down you went, remembering that you were facing downwards, swinging on the rope, gathering speed and using your legs to run down the cliff, controlling your speed by pulling back on your rope. It was frightening until you knew that the rope had got you, and then it became quite enjoyable. But watching others it was still very scary.

There were those who froze at the top and it took a fair amount of time to get their momentum going. But at the end of the day you knew that one way or another, it had to be done. It took two days to get everyone through.

As a matter of interest it was great cooking your own food on a Hexaman burner. The quality of the compo ration was good and tasty. At the end of the second day it was back to Bickleigh. When we got back to camp that evening, we heard through the grapevine that the War Cabinet was sitting in London over the Suez problem, and that 42 Commando RM had been put on standby. We hadn't been told anything official. After the weekend had gone by with various buzzes going around, there was still nothing really concrete.

Monday brought 650 squad to more serious work in Bickleigh Vale and Tor. After breakfast the squad was doubled down Heartbreak Hill to the river in the vale. The level of water was very high and flowing very fast - remember no health and safety at that time.

It was time for this week's rope cross and regain/recover. The rope was permanently fixed both sides of the river. The instructors checked it for any damage and for safety, in case vandals had damaged it. The crossing was about cricket pitch length, twenty yards or so.

The idea was that you got on to the rope chest down, with one leg dangling and the other leg hooked across the rope, and then used your arms to pull yourself across. On the other side the person who went before you then went back. Half way across you had to deliberately release your legs and hang from your arms, followed by the regain, which meant swinging your legs back on to the rope, making sure that you were facing the right way so that you could finish the crossing. If you didn't get your regain very quickly fatigue would set in rapidly, and that meant a dip in the river, which meant you were cold and wet for the rest of the day. The instructors knew everyone was going to do it again tomorrow, so they were in no hurry to make you do it again straight away.

After the rope crossing we had to go round the small lane to the top of the hill, where the start of the death slide was. The instructors were at the top and bottom of the slide. The one at the top would hand you a loop of rope, which was about 24 inches long. You put your hand through one of the loops, put the looped rope over the death slide and then put your other hand through the loop and grip. Taking your feet off the ground, your weight immediately closed the loops over your wrists so that you were locked into the loop. A push off by the instructor and down you went at a fair old lick through the trees, hanging straight down and looking straight ahead. As you approached the end of the slide, the instructor at the bottom had a length of rope over the slide rope which acted as a brake. It was a good job he was there, as you were going so fast you might otherwise have to be dug out of the ground.

These last two phases were to boost self-confidence and help to overcome fear. Like most dangerous but exciting experiences, after the first time you wanted more, and we were going to get lots more.

It was time to go back to camp for lunch, which meant

of course, the climb up Heartbreak Hill. The more you went up it the more significant the name became. To run up it even after the relatively light physical morning we had just had was extreme. To get up it at the double after a nine-miler, for example, would be impossible. It was the ultimate test of one's fitness and mental determination.

After lunch it was time to tackle Bickleigh Tor. Doubling out of the gate and down the hill, there was a two-mile run along Bickleigh Lane, and then at the end of the lane where it turned left we carried straight on into the woods. The Tor was covered in trees, but after many years of pounding boots there were well-worn tracks leading upwards. The Tor was a one-in-three climb for over a thousand feet, and even when walking up it you were bent over your knees. Occasionally you could get into a jog.

When you got to the top you emerged out of the trees and on to a plateau, in the centre of which was a large upright rock buried and isolated. It had obviously been put there by Royal. It was a tradition to touch it and run around it before descending. At the bottom we would regroup, fall in to ranks and commence the journey back to camp, visualising that climb up the hill.

This was a daily routine that went on for a number of weeks, until the end of August 1956. Although the training was very hard it was carried out in a much more relaxed atmosphere. The instructors were living in harsh conditions and pretty much knew that we were almost in sight of the finishing line. Then one day the Sergeant Major fell us in on the parade ground, because he said the CO wanted to address us.

When the CO arrived, he stood on a dais and asked if we could all hear him. At this stage we had no idea what was coming next.

"First of all I want to bring you up to date on the MOD's decision with regard to the Middle East" he said. "We, 42 Commando RM and 3 Commando Bde Headquarters have been put on standby to go to the Mediterranean island of Malta to train and acclimatise and to be closer to the area in question. It therefore has been decided to cut your training short by two weeks. At the end of this week, those of you the instructors know are ready to pass will do so and will be awarded their green berets. As of Friday, you will all then join 42 CDO RM as first class marines.

"The unit is to go on leave for two weeks. Those of you who are under the age of consent will get your parents' permission to go into combat if required. When you return from leave, if you have not already been recalled, that is when you will move to the Med, as and when. Good luck with the remainder of this week's training and I'll see you on Friday, all being well, to present you with your coveted green berets."

We were totally gobsmacked. The Sergeant Major wanted some details about beret sizes and addresses where we would be on leave. It was imperative that the unit knew at all times where you were, so you had to make a phone call to the rear party sergeant major if there was any change of details. Imagine the buzz and excitement in the squad following this very sudden change in fortunes. I don't know if it was just me, but I felt a sense of disappointment that we had not completed the full training period. But it was two weeks or so and we could be in a combat scenario in that period, so let's not feel downgraded in our achievement of the green berets - they were fully justified and very well earned. I say well done to all.

The next two days we were all spring-heeled. On the Friday, at a fairly low-key ceremony, we were all awarded our green berets and our shoulder flashes (Royal Marines Commando and Dagger). It was the proudest moment of my life, as I believe it was for everyone. I would have loved Mum and brother Jim to have seen it all.

That evening was spent sewing on the shoulder flashes to our battle dress tops, making sure they were lined up correctly. At least we could make comparisons with each other to get it right. When finished they did look impressive.

On the Monday morning, with all our kit, we were marched across to the 42 Cdo lines and handed over to the RSM. This was the end of the 650 Squad. We were separated into small groups and sent across to the various company sergeant majors. With five others I went to L Company with Captain Oakley and my troop commander, Lieutenant Hudson.

Once again we had to get settled into new accommodation, but it seemed hardly worth unpacking because we were going on leave on Friday. I thought it was worth stowing my kit away neatly to preserve it, rather than have it scrunched up in a kitbag for so many weeks. Hardly any of it was going to go on leave with me.

We were to travel on leave in uniform with one small suitcase. But before that, there was a lot of administration to be carried out by the Company Sergeant Major - passport applications, ID cards, leave passes, four weeks' pay and leave address details, travel warrants and vaccinations and inoculations as well as a medical check-up. Suddenly life was going by very quickly.

That night I thought about what I would do on leave. First, though, I tried to fathom out why my stepmother Edith had been so against me. She hadn't shown any interest in my school activities and had always made me walk to school sports matches. Very often I would have to run the three miles to Eton Manor to play for the school and then run home afterwards. I even had a chance to represent Essex county schoolboys at cricket - apparently Trevor Bailey had asked the school if I was good enough. The school sports master acknowledged that I was and asked my stepmother for permission for me to play. It was denied, I think because it would involve the expense of purchasing cricket whites etc for me. That bit I could understand, but not her antagonistic attitude to me. As far as my own mother was concerned, I still felt like asking why she had left us. Maybe I thought I might get some answers when I went on leave by spending some time with mother's sisters Aunty Doll and Aunty Vera at Bow. At that point I fell asleep.

Friday arrived and there was a mass exodus of ranks from Bickleigh. The local bus company had laid on extra coaches to get the lads to Plymouth station. My squad mate Nutty Edwards was travelling to London as well, so we started our journey together by catching the 11 am train to Waterloo. This time we were free to wander the train and have some lunch in the restaurant car. I felt very fit and proud as I discussed with Nutty at the table what he felt about the last nine months of activity. He said it all seemed a bit of a blur, all the pains and stiff muscles seemed as though they had never happened. We tried to remember all the laughs we had had and the good times.

We had a good journey up to the 'smoke', and when we arrived I said cheerio to Nutty, said I would see him in two weeks and told him to have a good leave and enjoy it.

It was my intention to visit all the aunts and uncles in Bow and Mile End before going to Leyton, Dad's place. At Waterloo I looked up the telephone numbers of everybody, not even knowing if they were on the 'dog and bone'. I couldn't get any information from the telephone directory, so I had to take pot luck. Knowing my aunties, they wouldn't hesitate to put me up for a couple of days.

It was my lucky day, because Aunty Doll was at home with Nan, and they welcomed me with open arms, I spent a week with them. Aunty Vera, who I liked very much, came round to talk to me about Mum, her sister Alice, although she gave me the impression that what had caused her death wasn't really known. At the end of the day it was put down to childbirth. My investigations later in life revealed that Mum had contracted rheumatic fever, which later led to dropsy and heart failure. Apparently dropsy wasn't spoken about very much in those days, because it had other connotations. I can see why a few years later Lavinia and Betty had left home in Leyton to come and live with the aunties at Bow before they went on to get married.

I can understand why my sisters decided to come and live at Bow. If they wanted peace of mind to go through the difficult times of being a teenager and a girl to boot, then the atmosphere in Antil road was as good as you were going to get anywhere in the East End. The people were absolutely wonderful, full of life and generosity, but the most striking thing of all was that they were genuine.

Aunty Doll and Uncle Pat seemed to have children coming out of their ears, though my memory cannot tell me if they were all theirs or whether they just fed the whole street. In my very early memory Uncle Bill was a lot of fun with Aunty Vera, and then suddenly he wasn't there any more. I know that we Collinses didn't get down to Bow very often, but it was great to be there on this occasion as a man.

While I was in the East End it struck me that the "Cockney Commando" had been born here and had come back to where it had all begun, Whitechapel, London. Would we see or hear of him again? Who knows?

CHAPTER SEVEN

It would soon be time for me to return from my leave. I had spent some time with Dad and my stepmum and managed to fit in a visit to Granddad Collins, but couldn't find out where my brother Jim was. He could have been in Aldershot or Egypt for all I knew. I wanted to call back to Bow to say goodbye to my mother's family, my Aunty Doll, Aunty Vera and their mother Mary and possibly their brother, Uncle Jim, but the chances of seeing them all together were pretty remote. I knew Aunty Doll was nearly always at home because she looked after Nan and therefore never went very far away from home. I did manage to see them and said my farewells over one of Aunty's famous bacon sandwiches cooked in real dripping.

I noticed that the front room was very empty, in comparison to the days when Uncle Pat had been proactive on Pickfords' lorries. In those days the room was always full of gear, as Uncle Pat called it, which had fallen off the back of other fleet vehicles. The police obviously loved him, because they were always visiting him!

I then went round to Aunty Vera's, she was a lovely lady. I was hoping to see Uncle Bill as well, another person I liked very much. But I was out of luck, there was no one at home.

It was time to return from my leave after a lovely time seeing them all. They were very impressed and proud of my achievement. I was now a Royal Marine in a fighting company and about to go overseas. But first I had to get back to Bickleigh before midnight the next day, when my leave pass expired.

Once again I had to get to Waterloo. Dad decided to travel with me on his way to work to Liverpool Street and said his goodbyes on the train. He had given his permission for me to go into combat if required, and I had his letter of approval. At Liverpool Street we shook hands, and he wished me all the best of luck in the world.

At Waterloo Station I looked around to see if there were any of the lads on their way back, but I couldn't see any. I had about an hour to spare before the train to Plymouth was due to leave, so I went across to the station restaurant for a bit of breakfast. A lovely young lady took my order and money, and brought my meal across to me. She gave me a lovely smile and I thanked her for the service.

I was pretty hungry and got stuck in with gusto. When I was about halfway through the meal, I noticed that two Royal Marines had come in. They had green lanyards, which meant they were HQ 3 Cdo Bde, and our CO had already told us that HQ would be going to Malta with us. They acknowledged me and I said hello to them, but they seemed to want to be on their own. Seeing these two lads, I had to keep reminding myself that I was no longer a recruit, I was one of the boys.

It was time to go across to Platform 5, board the train

and get comfortable and settle down for the journey, maybe have a sleep. The journey was uneventful, and no one joined me in the carriage. I knew I was going back to camp a day early, so I suppose that was why the journey was very quiet.

On arrival at Plymouth Station, I wondered if I should stay at the Navy Club overnight and travel to Bickleigh in the morning, but I decided against that and went straight to the bus depot to get the Tavistock bus, which went past Bickleigh Lane. That meant a fair walk down the lane, but as it turned out it was my lucky day. A Land Rover was coming down the road and the driver pulled over to give me a lift. "Cheers mate", I said. He told me that he had just driven from Plymouth Barracks, where there was a lot of activity going on in preparation for the move.

I showed my ID card at the gate and reported to the rear party office, handing in my leave pass. Only two other lads had arrived back into L Company lines, so it was a quiet return to my bed space. I unpacked my suitcase and stowed everything away, then I had a smashing hot shower. The accommodation block in 42 Cdo lines were very new and pretty luxurious in comparison to CTC across the other side.

I went across and read company orders, and found that I had been assigned to Lieutenant Hudson as his MOA radio operator. That meant that whenever the unit was in the field or in battle, I would be alongside him at all times, relaying and receiving his signals and messages and generally keeping an eye on him and his kit.

Now I knew my knowledge of radio and signal work was almost negligible, so I decided to report to Lieutenant Hudson on Monday and ask him if I could have some time with signal troop before we embarked to go abroad. I wanted to point out that just having finished training, my knowledge of signals work was limited. According to L. Company orders, we were to fall in on Monday morning at 0755hrs outside the company office. But I still had Sunday free, and I intended to make the most of my free time.

Having just come off leave and enjoyed the benefits of London's hospitality, I thought I should go for a jog down the hill to Bickleigh Vale and see if I could double up the hill, without any real pressure. It still felt as daunting as it had a few weeks earlier. I did pretty well, but didn't quite make it to the top. But boy, it was hard and it took a lot out of me. The guy on duty at the gate said, "You crazy fool!" and I agreed with him.

More and more of the lads were returning to the camp from leave. There was a hubbub of activity in the rooms and lots of stories about leave. Those lads from up north really did know how to enjoy themselves and some of the stories reflected that. Good luck to them.

Over the next few weeks the unit was involved in preparation for our stay in Malta. We were issued with what was called tropical gear, lightweight khaki shirts and shorts, and given a list of all the items we should take with us. Our heavy uniforms, greatcoats, blues etc, were packed and put into storage. I managed to get in some training time with signals troop so that I was now at least proficient enough to feel more confident on the radio.

It was decided that because we were going into combat at some stage soon and not being 100% sure of whether we were taking Suez by storm in helicopters or landing craft, we should carry out helicopter ditching and escape drills at Devonport Dockyard water tank. The simulated helicopter body was packed with about 10 or 12 Royal Marines who were strapped in. The body of the helicopter was then lowered by crane to the bottom of the tank and then rolled over on to its side. Everyone then had to unstrap their seat belt, remember which exit point was theirs and in an orderly fashion make their way out.

Two things were very important. Firstly you had to make sure that you got a good lungfull of air, and secondly not to panic if something went slightly wrong. It was one of those situations where you relied totally on each other. It was not something I would like to do every day, but it had to be done this time, at least once, to experience what the real thing might be like.

The date for the move had been decided by the powers that be, and before we knew it we were boarding naval coaches to be taken to Devonport dockyard. Most of the unit would be on board HMS *Cumberland*, with others on *Anzio* and *Reggio*. I believe they were called LPDs. It was a very tight squeeze on board, but we all knew it wouldn't take much more than five days to get to Malta, unless the weather in the Bay of Biscay was very bad.

On board there were bodies everywhere, on camp

beds, in sleeping bags, in hammocks and the lucky ones in cabins. Before you had time to settle down and discover where everything was on board, the ship was already steaming out to sea.

For me as a first-time sailor, not even qualified in ferries or rowing boats, I didn't know how I was going to take this trip. I had heard that crossing the Bay of Biscay could rate from fairly to very rough, or even worse. But so far I felt all right and I decided to go up top and have a look around. Most of 650 Squad were on board somewhere and I managed to find some of them. Dinger Bell, Sandy Powell, Alex Murphy and little Tich Ward were all up top. Remember in those days nearly everyone smoked and quite heavily too. Now that the ship was out of British territorial waters we could get duty free naval cigarettes and tobacco from the NAAFI shop on board. If I remember rightly, the cigarettes came in round tins. So I stayed with the boys for some time up top. We hadn't been able to meet up in the last week or so in Bickleigh because of the hectic pace of preparation. I thought that maybe when we got to Malta things might change, but I didn't bank on it.

With my new-found knowledge of signals procedures, it was a good time on board to join up with the other troops in L Company and get some practice time in.

I got through the Bay of Biscay reasonably well and found I was a fair sailor - at least I thought I was until I was told by a Naval Petty Officer that the Bay had been like a millpond. No wonder I didn't suffer much. I realised that if I had felt a bit rough, as long as I could get up on deck and view the horizon, the up and down motion wasn't half so bad. There were always others up there to chat to, to take your mind off of the swell. But some of the lads really did suffer.

The ship was now in the Mediterranean, past Gibraltar and into bronzie time, that's sunbathing to those who don't know. A running circuit around the upper deck had been laid out, so L Company had a session led by Lieutenant Hudson, in all about an hour. Then we had a weapon cleaning and handling period. The heavy weapons troop would have a bit of target practice. The ship's crew would put a target aft and tow it along, letting the boys let off controlled steam.

The following morning we arrived off Grand Harbour, Malta. It was early morning, so we waited outside to get permission to enter, dock and unload.

Transport was required to get the unit to the other end of the island, to Imtarfa Barracks on Rabat Hill. Eventually we went in to Grand Harbour and tied up at the bottom of Floriana. There were a number of naval buses, civilian buses and army three-ton trucks waiting for us on the dockside. It was brilliantly warm, at the end of the Maltese summer, and very comfortable for us. The local people had come out to view the arrival. The Maltese are very pro-British and a lovely race of people. For us youngsters this was paradise.

We hoped that at some stage we would be allowed to discover the island, but in the meantime it was back to the immediate business of being transported to Imtarfa. The Sergeant Major had us fell in with our kit, waiting to be told which vehicles were for us. But we were in no hurry. L Company ended up on naval coaches which took the middle road through the island, past Naxxar and Ta Qali airfield. This was the airfield where the Spitfires and Hurricanes had been based during the protection of Malta, when the island had won the George Cross. If you have seen the film *The Malta Story* you will understand what I am talking about.

Ahead of us we could now see Rabat and the Silent City. The buses climbed up the hill into and through Rabat and on to Imtarfa barracks. The famous hospital was over to the right, where many injured soldiers from the Desert Rats in North Africa, Navy and RAF personnel were taken care of. It was staffed by local VAD nurses and Queen Alexandra's nurses.

We dismounted on the parade ground and were shown to our accommodation block by the advance party which had come over a couple of weeks earlier. Of course they already had smashing sun tans and looked very well for it. We were in H Block, twenty to a room, ten down each side with a separate room on the end for the JNCO who would be responsible for discipline. The Sergeant Major said we had two days to get ourselves sorted, after which it was down to graft. Read orders tomorrow, he said, to find out what duties you are required to carry out. The galley staff that came out with the advance party had also recruited local cooks and workers, so we were going to be fed well. Our weapons were stowed away in the armoury.

As far as the accommodation block was concerned, each block had its own heads and washroom at the opposite end to the corporals' room. Although there was only one shower to twenty lads, it was a slow process, but then you didn't need hot water all the time in this temperature.

There was no shore leave for the time being, but there was a good cinema which was paid for and built by the Australians, just after the First World War. Cheers Aussies. There was a NAAFI staffed by local people, who would work day and night if required.

To me this place was heaven - peaceful, warm and very relaxing even when carrying out physical tasks. The whole environment was a joy. I loved the people, who were so nice and calm and polite, even after all the suffering of the fortress of Malta.

When we talked to the older generation of Malta, they spoke about the long and colourful history of the island. Some of the ladies still wore the ghonella, which was like a big black cape, I presume to keep cool. In Birkikara there was still a communal wash centre. It's very difficult to describe it, but it was a long series of very ornamental stone wash basins, with a natural supply of water where all the local ladies would carry out the weekly clothes wash. You really had to see it to understand fully what a lovely communal atmosphere there was. It was lovely talking to these old people, even for a young man like myself.

Because the summer had finished, we didn't need to use our desert khakis; our normal combat clothes, puttees and SV boots would be the dress. The following Monday was the first day of training in Malta, involving an acclimatisation run around Mosta, which meant running across farmers' fields and tracks. We were unkind to some of the farmers because the fields were full of grapevines, so we did a lot of scrumping of fresh grapes, wonderful. That was until "Malta dog" got us. The doc did warn us of stomach problems which always occurred with a change of water, bearing in mind that most of the fresh drinking water came from the sea, so it was always slightly salty. The return to Imtarfa up Rabat Hill was a reminder of Heartbreak Hill.

The old railway used to start at the back of Imtarfa, where the train used to run in to Valletta, but it had ceased to exist in the 1930s, when it became uneconomical to run because of the introduction of the bus company which covered more of the island. The old railway track was converted to roads.

From the top of the hill there was an outstanding view of Malta and in particular of Taqali's main runway and the devastation of the Hurricanes and biplanes as they had tried to protect the island during the last war, against overwhelming odds, from the Italians and Germans. Taqali was no more than a mud runway, not easy to negotiate after rain.

A visit to the military cemetery at Pembroke Lines will enlighten anyone to the tragedies of war, and in particular the loss of life of young children, sons and daughters of military personnel serving in Malta, North Africa and on board ships travelling through the Mediterranean at that time. The books and films since show about the bravery of all who served and lived on this small island, but they cannot show the full extent of what happened.

Back to reality. That evening we had a lecture from the intelligence officer about Egypt and in particular Port Said, which in fact was only about two days' sailing time from Malta. This meant we could do a dawn landing very rapidly, once the decision had been made.

But as yet the training went on. There was still to be no shore leave into Valletta, the capital of Malta, so the Company Commander of L Company decided his company should do some house clearing training at Ghajn Tuffieha. There was an old camp up there, so we spent a couple of days practising clearing houses. As you will see later the message didn't really get through to everyone.

Obviously things were warming up, because the CO decided that the unit should carry out a beach landing using Reggio and Anzio and their LVPs and LCPs. The beach to be used was the big and lovely bay at Mellieha, which was beautiful, a long approach into the bay.

We went on board early one morning and got round to Mellieha after a very sedate pace, just after lunch. It was decided that we would stay on board over night; we had compo rations so feeding wasn't a problem.

The landing was to take place at first light the next morning, giving us all time to practise boarding procedures. The landing craft crews also needed practice to get up to scratch. It didn't matter where we slept that night, so sleeping bags were the order of the day, down on the tank deck.

The following morning it was a struggle to get everyone washed and shaved, so we were up at 0330hrs and ready to carry out the assault landing at 0500. It was a glorious morning. I was wondering if the local residence had been warned what was about to happen, hoping that they had, because it could be quite a frightening scenario, especially just to wake up to it. It seemed that some people had got the message and were watching from the perimeters.

To us who were newly qualified, this was a brand new experience, but it was an essential training session. The CO said we might re-board and carry out a second loading and landing depending on the time. Come lunchtime it was decided that a second landing would take too long, so the transport that was going to pick us up from Grand Harbour was rerouted to Mellieha Bay. All the landing craft returned to their mother ships and practised a couple of reboards. Then the *Reggio* and *Anzio* set off back to Valletta.

We had some time to spare before the transport was due, so we all ate our compo rations just off the beach at Mellieha Bay. In relationship to Imtarfa we could have marched back, because we were at the right end of the island. But we decided not to, because the transport was on its way to us, and as it turned out it wasn't long before we were in transit to Imtarfa.

We had another week of exercises, training and acclimatisation. HQ 3 Cdo Bde were in St George's Barracks and were continually updating the plans for an invasion according to our CO, so the training went on.

The UK Government apparently had given the authority for the invasion to take place in 72 hours' time. We were told that a couple of warships had arrived in Grand Harbour, so the fleet was developing. We were to board the two assault ships in 24 hours' time, so it was flat out to get all the stores loaded. We were not going to take a lot of kit with us, a large backpack and a small kitbag which was going to stay on board in case of a long stay. From now on I was going to be in Lieutenant Hudson's back pocket.

To think that just twelve months before I had been a farmer's boy, and now I was a commando going in to battle. Frightening! Yes, I was going into battle with a radio and a 9mm sub machine gun. Lt Hudson would probably only have a 9mm pistol.

Once on board we would have a briefing from Captain Oakley, and then a few words from Lt Hudson directly to his troop. So why were we getting involved in Egypt's affairs yet again when British troops had recently been withdrawn from the Canal Zone? Well apparently Colonel Nasser had decided to nationalize the Suez Canal to help fund the Aswan Dam. We the British didn't support the project, in conjunction with the French and the Americans.

Colonel Nasser got to hear of the proposed invasion and blocked the canal with sunken ships and other debris. Eventually, after a lot of wrangling, as the French general wanted to do one thing and all the other generals wanted to be different, it was decided to make the attack at Port Said instead of Alexandria, with an Anglo–French force.

A plan was finally agreed. 40 and 42 Commandos would assault the beaches at Port Said, covered by a naval bombardment. 3 Para was to drop on Gamil airfield, with 45 Commando landing by helicopter some three miles inland from the assault beaches. The SBS had carried their normal pre-attack recce and would give their normal support. The French apparently were doing their own thing further down the canal.

There were still to be one or two changes to the plans, but our role as 42 Commando was pretty much the same as when we had first been briefed. A lot of what was going on was way over the heads of us young Marines on the ground. We were going to carry out our orders as briefed, so here we were now ready for the very frightening landing.

It seemed lately that we had been constantly on the move, with no time to get bored. This one was for real, and it was all going to happen after a good night's sleep, hopefully. I wasn't sure if I could relax enough to go to sleep. Everyone was buzzing around the company, probably in nervous anticipation. Eventually I went to sleep but I don't know what the time was, and I didn't get quality sleep.

We were woken up to be told that there was a 24hr delay. The whole fleet had sailed out of Grand Harbour during the night and was steaming east towards Egypt. After washing and shaving I went up top to see a panoramic view of many large ships, with lots of firepower. Naturally I had never seen anything like this before, well not in real life, perhaps on film, but this was different, this was very real. If and when that lot opened up, it would be very noisy. My thoughts went forward to the bombardment, and I hoped that I could cope and wouldn't let myself down.

After breakfast we were told to muster on the tank deck for an update of the situation. Captain Oakley briefed us on what was going to happen the following morning. We were told to expect heavy opposition on the beaches, which would have to be cleared before moving into town and fighting our way through to join up with the Paras, who were coming from the airfield which they should have secured earlier.

The bombardment of the beachhead would begin at 0400hrs and would continue for exactly one hour, when the assault troops would land on the beach, led by K and M Companies.

Lt Hudson told us to keep as busy as possible for the rest of the day, cleaning and oiling our weapons. We were to muster again at 1500hrs for the issue of ammunition and the filling of magazines. Having stowed all that away in our pouches, we picked up a 24-hour ration pack each and filled our water bottles. We were now basically ready for the off.

Up top it was getting dark, the fleet was on reduced lights and the big ships were hanging back almost out of sight. Once again, it was if you can sleep, then do so.

Those who were able to sleep were shaken awake at 0400hrs so as to get a good breakfast inside everyone, essential on a day like today. Suddenly all hell was let loose as the bombardment commenced from the ships out of sight. This was something special, as everything went over the top of us.

It was time for us to board our LTP, which was like a tank without a turret, open-topped with a ramp at the rear. The lads inside were facing backwards, Lt Hudson was in the cab with the cox/driver. L Company was to land after K and M Companies, who were going in by LCVPs, the traditional assault craft. After the initial work had been done by these two companies we would go through them into town and clear an area up to the Egyptian army camp, just the other side of Port Said.

The bombardment was still going on overhead, and I remember thinking to myself, surely there can't be anybody left on the beach?

I bet the naval gunners on board those big ships on the horizon were having a field day. To think that nothing was coming back in their direction.

The time was now 0445hrs, time for us all to leave the mother ship. The other two companies had already gone in the LCVPs and in five minutes, once the bombardment had stopped, would be landing on the beach to clear up.

As it turned out there was still a little resistance and we took some casualties. When L Company landed, we didn't have to get out of our craft and carried on through to the first built-up area. The resistance at first was light, so the company commander reassessed the situation and decided that if there was going to be any resistance it was going to come from the buildings ahead of us. So the order was -

out of the craft, and clear those blocks of flats. I relayed that message from Captain Oakley to Lieutenant Hudson.

Lieutenant Hudson and I went in to a block of flats with the rest of the troop spreading through the rooms. The building was clear, the occupants having presumably been frightened away by the bombardment. Personally, I felt a bit guilty going through someone's home with all their personal possessions lying around, considering that the individuals probably had nothing to do with the dispute, but were just ordinary families getting on with life. But this was something I had to accept.

So it was back down to ground level to watch the streets around our sector until all the clearing had been done and dusted. Our next move was back to the LTPs to move forward to the next sector.

As we moved up the road I saw some of K Company coming out the Egypt National Bank. I wondered if, as in the films, they were coming out with their pockets stuffed with banknotes. I had a little laugh to myself later on back on board *Reggio* when a message came through from the Commanding Officer to the effect that all monies seized in the assault, as well as any other souvenirs, weapons etc must be handed in. What a shame!

We progressed up the main central road. All seemed very quiet when suddenly we had the fright of our lives, or at least I did. Just after going past a side road on our right, a huge great tank lumbered out of the side road and swung round to face us and follow us. We blokes in the back were facing down the road and into the barrel of this monster.

I thought this was it. I believe my underpants changed colour.

There was nothing we could do but sit there. Suddenly Dinger Bell shouted, "It's OK, it's one of ours!" The tank had a letter H on the turret. It was definitely one of ours. At that time we didn't know the tanks had got ashore and this one was coming up from the beach. Phew! You really can start getting grey hairs at a very early age.

Two seconds later, a shot was fired from over on our right, the first shot in anger we had experienced. The round fizzed past my head and caught Dinger, who was sitting alongside me, a glancing blow on the left side of his face, just by his left eye. We didn't know what damage had been done at the time. The medic who was sitting directly behind Dinger realized what had happened and started to treat him.

Just then a second round came into the back and started to ricochet around the vehicle. I felt a burning sensation in my left leg, but didn't take any notice of it. I was more concerned about Dinger, whose blood was everywhere. I had blood on my left leg, but thought it was Dinger's. It turned out that a small piece of shrapnel had dug itself into my leg. It is still embedded there fifty years on.

Back to Dinger. The medic managed to stem the flow of blood, and he was conscious but in a lot of pain and shock. I signalled for a casevac (casualty evacuation), and the medic advised a chopper pickup at the army camp just up the road, once it was clear. Later we found out that Dinger had lost his eye, but was comfortable on board. He stayed with 42 Commando and was known as one-eyed Dinger. He was a very good footballer and carried on playing after the injury.

Now we were travelling very fast up the central road to the Egyptian army camp, where we thought there might be strong opposition. We spread out to work our way through the various barrack blocks. For some reason known only to him, Lieutenant Hudson decided to go off on his own - well not entirely, as I was with him. He was charging into rooms in what appeared to be in a total fearless fashion, with no regard for his safety or mine.

This was all getting rather out of hand and stupid. I was not going to let this rather exuberant young officer get himself - or me - killed because of his lack of care. I felt he was very gung-ho, and not very wise or professional. So I said to him, "Sir, I think you should slow down and enter these rooms with more caution. Remember the training at Ghajn Tuffieha. You have only got a pistol, if there's anyone in the room or it's booby-trapped you'll be taken out. Let's open the door and wait a moment, then we can go in together with a chance".

We compromised by going in together. As it turned out all the rooms we went in were empty. He smiled at me, but didn't say anything.

At this stage we couldn't see any of the rest of the troop. The troop sergeant had taken them to the right of us, and was moving much slower than us, with more caution. I can assure you that I matured very rapidly and probably aged as well. Lieutenant Hudson wanted to go back through the rooms to join up with the rest of the troop. I guided him round the outside of the buildings so that we were not confronted by our own lads still clearing. This way we could be seen clearly in the open by our own troops.

As we got to our starting point the sound of diving aircraft came from over our heads, just above the rooftops. Three RAF aircraft travelling at pace started firing rockets into the buildings behind us. We had not called them in, and had no knowledge as to why our own planes were firing so close to us and in the direction of our own troops. It turned out that some of 45 Cdo had been hit. I can tell you that didn't go down too well with us Royals.

Lt Hudson and I eventually joined up with the rest of the troop. A report from the troop sergeant indicated no contact, no casualties.

The conflict didn't last very long. The Paras had attracted the army from the barracks that we had just been through, and it appeared that the Egyptians had suffered heavy losses and captures. The Suez Canal had been blocked by the sinking of old ships at the Port Said end and these would take some time to clear. The governments were holding discussions about the invasion and the canal, so it was hoped that an agreement would be reached quickly. We certainly didn't want to be there any longer than necessary. From my personal point of view, to be initiated into battle in this way was quite frightening but in a way quite gentle.

Later that day we were ordered back on board to await the outcome and further orders. We stayed on board overnight and had some decent food, a shower and a good night's sleep. When we woke up the ship was on the move. It appeared that the whole thing had been called off and we were on our way back to Malta. The fighting had been stopped at midnight by the British Government. According to my records, on the 27th November 1956 I was awarded a Naval General Service medal for the Suez campaign.

So it was back to Imtarfa barracks, probably to stand by in case it all blew up again. But as it turned out all UK forces were withdrawn from the Suez area on 23rd December. My unit was to remain in Malta for the time being.

Having got back to a more steady routine, there was time for more sporting activities within the unit. Soccer was different out here, as there were no grass pitches and all games were played on compacted chalk pitches. Not good for goalkeepers or sliding tackles and the ball bounced very high. The local teams were very good at playing on this surface, and their control of the ball was out of this world. Now we had Dinger Bell back with us and he was very keen to get involved in playing and organising.

Captain Derek Oakley, our company commander, was a hockey and cricket man. Although the weather out here was great for cricket, there was only one cricket pitch on Malta and that was at Marsa, the other end of the island, so we didn't get so much involved even though we understand that there was a Malta team. It wasn't the cricket season, so the game was forgotten.

We were now heading towards Christmas, so lots of thoughts were going into party times, but physical training still had to go on to maintain standards.

It was mainly running up and down the hills that worked for us. Of course you never had very far to go for a good swim.

One morning I woke up feeling very unwell. The MO said I had a serious case of flu and immediately sent me to Imtarfa hospital with a temperature of about 104. I can tell you I really felt rough and didn't want to do anything at all, Christmas or not. For the first four days I think I was asleep. I know I was aching all over and shivering. But slowly I started to feel better and after a week I was sitting up looking for mischief.

I remember a young nurse came round one morning to take temperatures, at the same time as the tea lady came to give me a cup of Rosie Lee and put it on the side. I thought to myself I would play a little joke on the nurse. The thermometer was in my mouth, so I took it out and dipped it in the tea. I didn't realise just how hot the tea was and the thermometer just exploded, the mercury draining into the tea cup.

I had enough intelligence to realise that this was a dangerous situation, so I jumped out of bed, took the tea cup to the heads and drained it all away down the loo. I washed the cup out and went back to my bed, where the nurse was waiting and wondering what I was doing. I said I had dropped the thermometer on the floor and broken it and then gone to the heads to get a drink of water. She gave me a wry smile of disbelief and didn't pursue it. Matron was coming down the ward, so I jumped into bed, I didn't want the young nurse to get into trouble. I got away with a silly prank.

Although I was feeling a lot better, the episode of running around the ward really took it out of me. I wasn't ready for anything strenuous.

The MO said I could rejoin my unit in time for the New Year. The flu bug had drained me and I didn't feel very much like celebrating. There was a sort of bash over in the NAAFI, so I went over with the boys for a rum and coke. It tasted very good, but I thought it wise not to have another until midnight to bring in the New Year 1957. Sleep was creeping up on me.

CHAPTER EIGHT

At the start of New Year 1957, I was thinking very hard about my career in the Royal Marines. Should I stay as a general duties marine, or should I perhaps specialise?

The promotions prospects appeared to be a lot better in the specialist branch. I decided to train in the driver's branch and asked the Sergeant Major if I could apply for a D3 driving course. My application went ahead in Feb 1957.

I was hoping that I could stay in Malta for a while longer, because I loved it there. I hadn't yet got a summer in and wondered if after a driver's course I would get the chance to go back.

I was sent back to the UK in early February, to Portsmouth to be precise, to carry out the Driver 3 Course, which was to last ten weeks. The course consisted of driving Land Rovers, Humber 1 tons and Bedford MK 3 tons and learning about vehicle mechanics and maintenance. Of course, in between driving there were guard duties to be done in Eastney barracks at the main gate and at central points around the barracks. I got away with any ceremonial guards, as because of the Suez campaign my heavy kit was still in Bickleigh storage. The T Company Sergeant Major made a brave effort to get my kit to Portsmouth, but it never did arrive before my course finished.

With my driving experience on the farm, I passed the driving test on all vehicles comfortably. I had a few problems with the technical examinations, but managed to get enough marks. Then as a qualified D3 I was posted, can you believe it, to Lympstone, where I was to drive a three-ton truck taking new recruits to Woodbury and Dartmoor, doing the things I had been doing a year previously. I liked driving very much, and it was, as I discovered, something I was good at.

I spent the next six months at Lympstone learning the art of professional driving on UK roads. For the first time for a long time I was able to get back into cricket, though it took quite a few games for me to start to feel comfortable playing. I had an incentive in Cpl Fletcher, who was in our team and was also the Corps' main fast bowler at that time. As an out-of-practice fast bowler I had to make a distinct effort to match him and become the team's opening bowler. Though I say it myself, we became very successful and were feared by the local teams.

At the end of the season, around September, I was pleasantly surprised to be posted back to Malta to join the green lanyards of HQ 3 Cdo Bde. I was very lucky to be posted back to Malta, because I could have been sent anywhere in the UK. I counted my blessings, because I loved Malta.

The flight out of England was from Brize Norton, on board what I think was a Britannia aircraft. I'm not very good at aircraft recognition, but I believe it was a turbo prop aircraft, which made it quite modern. There weren't many people travelling, because there were only a few seats and quite a lot of cargo. Not that I was worried, my head was still buzzing at the way my life had been in the last twelve months. People would have paid a fortune to enjoy the experiences I had had. So much had gone on in such a short period; remember I wasn't yet twenty years of age.

We took off from Brize on a lovely sunny afternoon, expecting to arrive in Malta at about four o'clock local time. On board was a lady who was struggling with a new baby and her baggage. For some reason she was sitting on the floor of the craft. I could see that she was struggling with all her bits and pieces of baggage and the baby, so I asked if I could help in any way. She turned out to be the wife of Bob Euden, one of my Suez mates from 42 Commando. She was joining Bob in Malta because he was now with HQ as the Brigadier's MOA.

It appeared that since the Suez campaign there had been a lot more stability in the area, so families were allowed to join their husbands. This meant that the lads would now have the freedom to explore the island.

I had gained six months' driving experience in the UK, but none of that would have prepared me for driving on the roads in Malta. If you had experience on a skid pan, that would have helped more. Driving out here can be very difficult, with constant sunshine. The tarmac roads were polished like glass, and whenever it rained the surface became like ice. There was a lot of skill and experience to be gained in driving in those particular conditions. Military vehicles would generally be run on cross-country tyres throughout the year. This made matters worse in slippery conditions, but practising with care on ice made you a much better and more experienced driver.

The Motor Transport Officer apparently had me lined up to become the Brigadier's driver, when the existing driver was due to leave. Marine Thompson was a three-badge officer and was due to go home in about three months. He had been the Brigadier's driver for a long period, so once again a challenge for me. The MTO also thought I should carry out the junior command course before taking up the new appointment. The next course at Ghajn Tuffieha was in two weeks' time.

Because the commando units were staying on the island indefinitely, the old camp where we had carried out our house-clearing training had now been refurbished as the JNCO's cadre. The staff had been sent out from the UK training establishments. It looked as though the place was set to be for some time. So off I went to Ghajn Tuffieha for lots of parade work and weapon training.

When I got there, our instructor, can you believe it, was Sergeant Tyack from Deal. There was no instant recognition from him and I didn't expect there to be; it was business as usual, "get fell in over there!" In all there were about twenty lads from HQ, 45 Commando and 42 Commando who were still in Malta at that time.

The junior command course pushed you in a different way. You had to prove yourself able to take control of other men and difficult situations. I really wasn't sure of myself at this level. But everything had happened so quickly of late that I was into it up to my neck. Extra effort was required from me to get through.

Out the back of Ghajn Tuffieha camp is a beautiful sandy bay, so nearly every morning after breakfast the routine was to double through the camp and down the rocks to the beach for a swim. The cadre had some canoes down there, so some training went into that as well. Most of the time was spent on the parade shouting out orders and getting them in the right sequence.

There was a lot of fun to be had in the tasks procedures. You had to take control of half a dozen lads and planks of wood, with the aim of getting over a fence or obstacle without anyone touching the ground. Good fun.

There was a lot of starching, pressing and polishing, but at the end of four weeks we were lined up on parade and given the results. It was one of those courses where the instructors would have looked bad if you had failed, because everyone on the course was recommended to attend by a senior officer. Anyway, after some hard work by me, I made it.

I went back to the transport section as a lance corporal. I expected to lose my stripe, but I was told by the Transport Sergeant Major that I would keep it for the time being. I wasn't given a reason, but later I realised why.

I spent a week with Marine Thompson learning the Brigadier's routine and habits. Brigadier Houghton lived with his family in the big house at St Andrew's barracks, just up the road from where I was at St George's barracks.

I got the impression that the drivers' branch were very short of promotable ranks, because I was being pushed at all times. The next step for me would normally be the D2 course at Portsmouth, but having just arrived out there in Malta, there was no chance that I would get a course back in the UK for some time. I hoped this would mean that I could have a bit of quality time at work and on the island, with no more courses for a while. Perhaps I could get a bit of sports time in, as I hadn't played football for some time, so I had a chat with Dinger to see if there were any games on. There were only one or two internal matches being played, departmental mainly.

But all that was hit on the head when I was told that approval had been given for two Royal Marines to carry out the Army B2 course that takes place every so often here in Malta. The qualification, if passed, would be accepted as the equivalent to the Royal Marine D2 course. This was fast tracking at its best. The course was to begin in ten days' time in Floriana.

The course was brilliant, just the two of us, both Lance Corporals from the recent junior command course at Ghajn Tuffieha. We had our own driving instructor, who was with the RASC, and a Scammell recovery truck which was our main vehicle. It appeared to me that this course was equivalent to our D3 course with bigger vehicles. What we were being taught in the classroom was very similar to the technical side of the D3 course, including vehicle mechanics, a certain amount of administration, such as traffic accident procedure and stores documentation for vehicles.

I enjoyed the course and its relaxed atmosphere, especially the driving of the very big Scammell through the narrow streets of Floriana and Sliema. We seemed to get on very well with our instructor, who also seemed to be enjoying taking the course. It was a brilliant eight weeks, and we didn't seem to be under any pressure at all.

It was soon exam time. First the driving test and manoeuvres, which went very well and we both passed with flying colours. The written exams were to take place the following morning, so it was back to St George's barracks to carry out some revision in preparation for the morning. All the next morning was tied up with written exams. A lot of the papers were multiple-choice papers where you just ticked the right answer. I didn't find them too difficult, as a lot of the subject matter had been covered at Portsmouth.

We both passed with at least 75 per cent. The results were sent to the Promotions Office at Portsmouth, which acknowledged that we were now qualified D2.

Back to my duties as the Brigadier's driver. The unit was going on exercise to North Africa, all the way along the north coast, Tripoli, Sirte, Benghazi and Tobruk. This was going to be very exciting for me, because not only did the Brigadier take his Champ (a Jeep-style military vehicle), he was also taking the caravan. This was a one-ton enclosed vehicle decked out inside as an office and accommodation in the field. It would be most invaluable for my driving experience to go cross-country in soft sandy conditions, using sand channels, four-wheel drive and recovery duties. I was hoping the Brigadier would want to cover lots of miles. The caravan was parked in the HQ area at Homs.

The boss decided to have a day out in the desert, visiting a number of the battlefields of North Africa, where we found lots of knocked-out tanks and heavy guns. They were well preserved because of the very dry climate. The metal was not rusting or deteriorating at all, so one could imagine them staying there for some time.

We also spent a number of hours at the cemetery, which was looked after by the War Graves Commission, and I might say very well looked after. I then took the Brigadier back to Homs, because the exercise was due to finish the next day and he said he wanted to finalise things.

At the end of the next day all the vehicles went back to the docks to reload on to HMS *Anzio* and *Reggio*. I believe HMS *Bulwark* was in the area as well.

Once I got the Brigadier's Champ on board, I had to go back for the caravan, which was locked. I noticed that it was a lot heavier now than it had been when coming out. I was to find out why when we got back to St Andrew's.

It was a very short trip across the Mediterranean to Malta and very soon we were entering Grand Harbour. The view on entering the harbour always gives me a thrill; to me it is unique and gives one a real sense of history.

As we tied up, the customs officers came on board to check that we boys did not have too many duty-free items.

It was a cursory check, because the customs had a very good relationship with the commandos and I think they knew that some of these trips were rabbit runs.

I was told to take the caravan to the officers' mess to be unloaded, so I asked what had to be unloaded. Apparently the duty free in Tripoli and Homs was very much cheaper than in Malta, hard as it is to believe, so the trip across the water was always well worth it.

Having got the caravan back to St Andrew's, I left it there and went back to the ship to pick up the Champ and the Brigadier. On getting him home he said that he had no official functions for the next three days, so I could have the time off, which was nice. But I was always on call should he change his mind. He might decide to go in to work and need the car. But at least it gave me the chance to get my dhobi done and get up to date with my personal administration.

I also had the two vehicles to clean. The car was in good nick and had been garaged while we were away. The Champ needed a good clean to get rid of all the sand, but it wasn't too bad.

On the social side, before our trip to North Africa, I had been invited to a party at Marshall Court, which was the area the navy used as housing. Gordon Matthews, one of my driver mates, had a brother in the navy, and the party was at his place.

I was still very shy at parties, but getting better at it. I was a good listener, and my greatest fear was always someone asking me to dance. I still wasn't good at it, because I had had practice, bearing in mind my philosophy, that if you are good at something then you don't mind people watching, so the reverse also applies. If you know that you are no good at something then you avoid it no matter what it is.

I noticed two lovely girls at the party, who seemed to be together. Gordon's brother introduced me to them, Marianne and Rose, sisters who live very close to Marshall Court. I noticed that Marianne in particular had lovely legs as well as a beautiful face. Her sister Rose could almost be taken as her twin.

When Marianne found out that I was a commando, it brought back a warning from her father. "Beware of commandos, they are dangerous!" he had said. The warning made her want to find out why we were considered dangerous!

Before the party was over I asked Marianne if I could meet her again. She told me that her father was very dominant and nearly always chaperoned the girls wherever they went together, so it would be difficult to meet up very often.

I don't know how we got away with it, but somehow we did have more dates and we got to know each other very well. Malta is a wonderful place for courting, with lots of cosy little bars and restaurants and weather you could rely on. There were lovely bays, coves and historical places to see.

As time went by, I eventually got permission to visit her parents and family. They were lovely people with a large family of boys and girls. One of the young boys, Dominic, who was deaf and dumb, was a lovely kid and football mad, so I spent a lot of time with him kicking a ball around on the waste ground near their house. He was unlucky that his mother had contracted German measles while carrying him. He got on very well with everybody, adapting and coping with lots of situations which even able-bodied people would struggle with.

Dominic used to come along to watch us play football when the Royal Marines played against Sliema Wanderers at Gzira Stadium. Sliema wasn't Dom's team, as he seriously supported the Greens of Floriana. He had an association with Floriana for the whole of his life, as it turned out, and was really loved by all of the players over the years.

The next eldest to Marianne, her brother Lawrence, had gone to England earlier on a scholarship-cum-employment as a civil servant in the Chatham dockyard.

One day I got very brave and asked Marianne if she would marry me, and to my surprise she said she would. We talked about when and decided that August of the following year (1959) would be a good time. The hot summer weather would be easing slightly and I would be coming to the end of my time in Malta. I asked her father for his permission to get married, and he said yes.

Now because I was under 21, I had to get my dad's permission before the Royal Marines would consider it. I didn't think Dad would say no and he didn't. So the date was set for 8th August 1959 and to show that I was sincere,

The lads on our first shore leave in training, 1956 Exmouth.
AC, Powell, Milton, Meadows, Mudie and Kelly

1956 - just finished training and about to join 42 Cdo RM

1956 – section B Troop 42 CDO, Suez Centre, rear row is Bob Euden

3 Cdo Bde around the time of the Suez Campaign, early 1957

As the Brigadier's driver, 1958

My best man and best friend Gerry escorts me to the church, just in case I chicken out

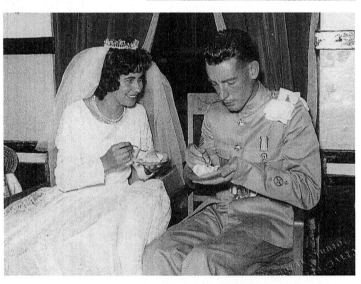

A very happy day for us all – our wedding day, August 1959 on the lovely island of Malta

The sisters Rose and Marianne in reflective mood. Just parted for the first time in their lives

Now its your turn Gerry. About a year later. Sorry I couldn't be with you.

I had lessons and converted my religion to Roman Catholic, something that Marianne's parents really wanted, because of the faith of any future children. The Maltese people at that time were very religious.

My promotion to substantive corporal came through in early 1959. I couldn't really believe it, just three years after joining at Deal. According to everything I had heard, you had to wait for dead men's shoes to get promoted in the Royal Marines. I must have joined at the right time.

This meant of course that I would lose my job as the Brigadier's driver, because as a JNCO I would be expected to have a lot more responsibility than just driving an officer around. So now I had a transport section of my own and there was no going back. I was on the promotion ladder, which meant more courses and study. First of all I had to get the higher education exam, which would take me as far as Sergeant Major. But all that was in the future and back in the UK.

Having recently got back from the exercise, the combined services were invited to play football against local sides. One fixture that always stayed in my memory was the annual game against Sliema Wanderers FC in the Gzira stadium. As I have mentioned before, all soccer pitches there at that time were chalk-based. The British way of playing soccer was not suited to hard grounds, and we didn't have the skills to control the ball, thus the game.

Maurice Walsh was the star of Malta and Sliema, and he used to make us look rather amateurish with his ball control and slick passing. Although we were much fitter than the local lads, our energy was used up chasing the ball. It was always a great game of football, and local spectators, including Marianne's brother Dominic, always enjoyed the game.

Ironically, Maurice ended up as a family member. He married the sister of John, who married Marianne's sister Josephine. A bit complicated, but a relation nonetheless. Dinger Bell was our team captain and to this day in Malta there are fond memories of one-eyed Dinger and his team.

We had a lovely wedding in Gzira church with the reception in a private villa in Sliema, all thanks to Marianne's parents. A number of my Royal Marine friends and bosses came to the wedding. My best man was Gerry Bourne, a driver mate of mine. I had no hesitation or second thoughts about choosing Gerry. He was a nice guy, full of laughter and fun. He took a fancy to Rose, but she was already spoken for by a local lad, Emmy.

Gerry and I spent a lot of time together. We were great mates, living in the same barrack room. Also in our group were Darby Allen and Sharkey Ward, both in my transport section. All four of us seemed to gel together. We didn't go ashore a lot but seemed to be able to find plenty of fun around the perimeter of the barracks, which had the sea on two sides of it, so we would mess about on the rocks. These lads were really quite sensible for nineteen-year-olds. We believed that being in Malta was an ideal time to save money and to boost the bank balance.

When together on the rocks we would even attempt to go fishing, not with proper gear but with made-up rods and bread for bait. Schoolboy stuff really. We would sunbathe on the flat roof of our room. But the biggest laugh of all was our attempt at being the Lonnie Donegan skiffle group. We could sing the songs, but when it came to the instruments we were a bit limited. I had a guitar but could only play a couple of chords. Gerry had a tea chest bass with one string, Darby from somewhere had a washboard and Sharkey sort-of played the mouth organ. We were pretty grim, and the rest of the lads in the room would scarper at the first note, but we had a lot of fun trying. We didn't take it too seriously. We knew we were useless.

It was a lovely wedding. Of course we couldn't go off the island for a honeymoon, but we were going to England very shortly.

That evening after the reception, without appearing to be in too much of a hurry, we said goodbye and thank you to everybody and went off to the flat we had arranged for the remaining few weeks of our time in Malta. We had a hire car available to us, arranged by a family member who had a garage.

Opening the door of the flat and entering our new home with my lovely wife gave me the most wonderful feeling of excitement I had ever experienced in my life. To be totally alone, the two of us, with no one to look out for, no father-in-law, no rules and regulations to worry about – it was total freedom. These moments were of extreme pleasure, something to treasure and remember for ever.

Our first couple of days after the wedding were spent relaxing at the military lido in St George's Bay. It was a treasured time of freedom and pleasure in each other's company. Marianne loved swimming and she was brilliant at it, not a duffer like me. We were able to take her brothers and sisters with us to the Lido.

On the second day while swimming, Marianne gave a shout of anxiety. I thought she had been stung by a jellyfish or some such creature. Then she called me to say that her wedding ring had come off her finger and had sunk to the bottom of the sea, about 15 to 20 feet down. Poor Marianne had tears in her eyes. I tried to console her by telling her that I would get another one, but I knew it wouldn't be the same.

The chances of finding the ring were very remote, because the sea bed was a mass of rocky crevices, but I decided that we would give it a try. There were a couple of young lads with snorkel gear, who said they would give us some help. They went down a couple of times, with no success. I also went down, but having seen the sea bed I realised that the chances were nil. But as a group we kept looking, because Marianne was distraught.

Then one of the boys suddenly came up screaming with joy. He said that as he had been swimming around, he had seen the ring sitting on a small rock, as though it had been placed there. A chance in a million. Even more amazing was the fact that it could be seen from above. I couldn't thank the boys enough for their efforts. Both Marianne and I felt very thankful and relieved that Lady Luck was on our side.

We spent the next few weeks relaxing around the

island, visiting and saying our farewells to relatives. It was a very happy ending to my tour of Malta. I suppose I had to top up my sun tan before going back to the UK, as after two years out here it was expected.

CHAPTER NINE

Finally my tour of duty with HQ 3 Cdo Bde was at an end and Marianne and I were to leave Malta. On the big day, it seemed that half the island had come to Luqa airport to see us off. For Marianne it was going to be a very new life and a bit of a culture shock, without the very close-knit family bonds she had been used to. I was sure she was going to miss her sister Rose deeply, because they had been so close growing up.

Marianne was a really beautiful lady, and I was going to have to watch and protect her very carefully, especially at Royal Marine functions.

The social life in the forces is really something special. The motto 'work hard and play hard' certainly applies. I always wanted to give her the best I could afford, and if that meant getting promoted, then that's what I would do.

My next posting was once again to Lympstone, but before that I had a few weeks' leave. It was time for me to show off my lovely wife in London. We stayed in Leyton for a while and while there we went up to the city to see some of the sights. On a lovely day we went to the Serpentine and rowed around the lake.

A visit to Bow was another must. The aunties down

that way fell head over heels in love with Marianne and thought she was adorable, as of course she was. Aunty Vera now had Peter and Graham; she had been carrying Graham the last time I had been there.

We soon had to make our way down to Devon, and remember in those days very few people had a car and as yet I couldn't afford to buy one. So it was a train journey for Marianne and me to Exmouth, which was a first for her. I think the Malta train had ceased to function around the time Marianne was born. A large suitcase travelled with each of us, with all our worldly possessions and clothing.

As a corporal, life was going to be easier at work, but finding accommodation as newly-weds wasn't easy. A married quarter would come in due course, but initially private accommodation, at any rate good private accommodation, was difficult to find. Eventually however we found a nice place in Exmouth. It was an upstairs flat in a very large house in excellent condition, not too far from the shops, but a very long walk to the Catholic church. Maybe once a week we could manage it. Marianne was happy there, even though she was being left on her own while I was at work.

Then - wonderful news. Marianne was expecting a child, due in June 1960. The house we were in was very suitable for three of us. We couldn't have been happier preparing for the new arrival and shopping around for baby stuff. We bought a lovely Pedigree sprung pram, a fine cot and lots of baby clothes. In those days it was all pot luck as to whether it was a boy or girl, so colour selection was all in the mind. Everything that we got was blue. Was this wishful thinking?

Marianne decided that she was going to have the baby at home. My poor wife suffered with morning sickness, and at that time there was a new medication for morning sickness, called Thalidomide. I believe Marianne said that she tried it once only, thank goodness, because it turned out to be the cause of hundreds of children being born severely disabled with missing or deformed limbs. Of course at the time there was no knowledge of the severe danger, so we were very lucky that Marianne made that brave decision not to take it, and to suffer the sickness instead.

The midwife said having the baby at home would be OK, but the bed had to be put up on blocks to a suitable height for the midwife to work. What a wonderful time it was, waiting for the moment.

Finally, when June arrived, so did our little daughter Denise Marie. I was determined to be there, and what an experience it was for me. I can remember distinctly the midwife saying to Marianne "Do you want some oxygen?" The oxygen was in a canister beside the bed. Marianne was gripping my hand so tightly that her fingernails were digging into my flesh and causing the hand to bleed. I was trying to be so brave. I lifted the canister on to the edge of the bed.

"I don't want that!" she screamed, and threw the canister across the room. "I want my mum!"

What a lovely baby Denise was. Once again I felt so proud. This was even better than receiving my green beret.

The big teddy bear we had bought her was sitting in the armchair, and I think fifty years later she still has it.

I was on compassionate leave for two weeks to be at home with Marianne while she recovered. I must admit she was a very strong lady. Baby Denise was born in perfect condition, thank goodness.

With no car we walked everywhere, and I can tell you that for a man, especially me, wheeling that big pram around Exmouth and having people stopping to have a look at the baby was a thrill.

Soon after Denise arrived we were awarded a married quarter in Trafalgar Road in the village of Lympstone. It was a smashing house, with a very large back garden, and can you believe it - our next-door neighbour was a lady from Malta. Her name was Ephros, and she was married to a corporal in the barracks. This was good news for Marianne, because I was due to start my four-week SNCO's course. Although the course was at Lympstone, I would have to work all sorts of hours. But we had time together to get settled in to the new house before the course began.

I was hoping that we could be settled in Lympstone for a long period, and enjoy the time as a young family. But first of all I had to get this next course out of the way. Once again it was like all promotion courses, lots of time on the parade ground and a lot more practice at preparing and delivering lectures covering all sorts of subjects, military and general knowledge. As an SNCO, you were expected to be well able to instruct officers senior and junior and advise where necessary, and you had to be able to assess the standards of the lads who were on the promotion list and write reports on them.

The course went very well from my point of view. I struggled a little yet again on the parade ground, as I don't like being a drill instructor. You have to be a special breed to wield a pay stick.

I passed with flying colours, and then it was back to my daily duties in the transport department for a while. This meant I could get home pretty much on time every day, except if I was on duty in the regulating office of the MT.

One of our sergeants in the transport section was Charlie Tee, who also lived in Trafalgar Road. Marianne and I got to know him and his wife Lilian very well, because Charlie played cricket for the unit and the sergeants' mess.

Cpl Fletcher was still at Lympstone and when he found out I was back in camp he immediately signed me back up for the unit. Most of the matches for the season had been played and the weather was beginning to change to football and rugby conditions.

Marianne got on well with Charlie and Lilian and we were invited to their house whenever he had a dinner party. This meant a babysitter, and Ephros and Marianne shared these duties.

Then I was told I had been selected for the drivers' first class course at Fort Cumberland, Portsmouth, beginning in three weeks' time. That would mean I would be away from home for eight weeks, I hoped I would be able to get home on some weekends. In the meantime Charlie and his wife invited us to a dinner party the following week. I wasn't keen, but with him being one of my bosses I suppose we had to go. However I was becoming more aware of Marianne's reluctance to go to these kinds of parties. I could fully understand her feelings, mainly because of the adult games that were often played. She was now getting somewhat jealous of any interest being shown in me by other women. I was aware of this and tried my hardest to protect her from any situation that I knew would upset her.

On this particular occasion, a game was being played which involved someone being nominated to wait outside the room in the hall. The loser of the game would have to go out into the hall, to put with whatever happened.

Sure enough it was inevitable that I would get sent out of the room when Charlie's wife was in the hall. I had a plan in my mind for what to do if this happened, a plan which I thought would protect Marianne's feelings. I had decided to go upstairs to the loo, so that there was no chance of contact with Lilian, should she want to make any. But it misfired on me, because I was away for much longer than the others who had gone out, and it totally backfired. When I went back down and entered the room, everyone clapped and commented how long I had taken. I was hoping that Lilian would explain and come to my rescue, but she didn't.

Marianne appeared to be upset, so I knew it had affected her. I tried to explain to her what had happened, and that in trying to protect her, it had all gone very wrong. Once again I was the innocent party being blamed for something I hadn't done. Have you heard that before?

Having experienced that situation, I became even more cautious and aware of delicate situations. I realised that jealousy could be very hurtful and dangerous.

I loved Marianne deeply, and would do everything in my power to protect her. I thought perhaps the way to prevent sensitive situations was to turn down invitations to social events. But as I was going away for some time, the problem was not going to occur.

It was now time for me to go off to Portsmouth to start my D1s course. This was an in-depth course, not so much involving driving skills but more in the skills of communication, lecturing, mechanics, motor-cycling and administration, including stores demanding and invoicing. We also had to cover waterproofing of vehicles and the testing of those vehicles.

On arrival at Eastney Barracks I was accommodated in the main block with all the other corporals on the course. I was very pleasantly surprised to find that I was by far the youngest on the course. I am not sure if that fact was going to help me in any way, as these other lads would have a lot more experience than me. This was an incentive for me to push myself to the limit. I would have liked more driving on the course, but then if you couldn't drive properly now then you shouldn't have been selected to do the course.

My ability to study and absorb information was getting

much better, so I was more confident in my ability to pass the course. It was a very interesting course and one that was essential for future promotion. There were no more technical qualifications I would need before becoming a sergeant major, so this was a must and I had to ensure I gave it all my attention.

I was able to get home for a couple of weekends, and it was lovely to see and be with the family and to know that they were all very well. Marianne said it had been a great help to have Ephros living next door. The weekends absolutely flew past, and I wouldn't have missed one of them.

The course was going very well, but the answer was going to come at the end with a number of tests and exams. I was hoping I could get home for Denise's first birthday the next weekend, but it was touch and go because we were in the last two weeks of the course and I didn't want to jeopardize my chances. But luck was with me, one of the other corporals was going back to Plymouth in his car and he said he would drop me off at Lympstone and pick me up from there on Sunday early evening.

This was great news and brilliant of him to offer. I helped out with the fuel costs, and we were able to leave Eastney at tea time on the Friday. Marianne was very surprised to see me.

At the end of the course I was informed of my next move, which came through a bit sooner than I would have hoped. 43 Cdo was being reformed and I was part of the plan. It was going to be Plymouth and Stonehouse barracks in September 1961.

I completed the D1 course successfully in July 1961, so we had a couple of months of relatively stable married life before the next move. The vegetables were growing well in the garden, so we could use some of those before we left. It was very close to our second wedding anniversary and our second child was due in October; by then we would be in the Plymouth area.

We never seemed to get a settled posting for any real length of time. I knew that the promotion system, the qualifications and the promotions ladder had been a big influence on my movements since arriving from Malta.

We were now on the move to a naval hiring in Devonport, but first we had to clean and return the married quarter here in Lympstone.

We were both still quite young and there was a buzz every time we got posted, all to do with the unknown, and we weren't quite sure what was coming next. But again it was time to say goodbye as we caught the train to Plymouth.

The naval hiring was in a place called St Budeaux, not the best of areas and not the best of accommodation, but at least we were moving in immediately and managed to get settled very quickly. The shopping area was just up the road, which was just as well, as we were slightly out on a limb. It didn't matter to us too much as we were getting very excited about the baby, which was due any time. Once again Marianne decided to have it at home, so we had a good idea of the routine, although the different midwives had different ideas.

Lovely Joanne Louise was born in October and all went very well. I managed to get some leave, which was a help to Marianne, because I could look after Denise for a bit and take her shopping. We still did not have a car, so it was a lot of walking for everyone.

I would have expected to be at Lympstone for at least two years, but that didn't work out. With the reforming of 43 Cdo I thought perhaps I was going to be there for some time, but I was finding it very difficult to understand why I or anybody else had been sent to Stonehouse Barracks. It appeared to me that everything was being done in slow motion. It was as if there was uncertainty that the plan for 43 Cdo was going ahead.

In the overall picture, I can perhaps understand that having recently qualified as D1 I would be well up to date with transport procedures and therefore could be of good value in setting up a transport section. But before I really knew it, I was told that I was being posted to Singapore to a new concept in transport, Transport and Composite. A troop was being formed in Nee Soon camp, to carry out logistic work for and on behalf of brigade units in Singapore and Malaya.

As time went by we got a little more excited about the move to Singapore, because I knew that a posting like this one meant at least three years out there. The only problem was that I was being sent alone, with the family to follow later. This meant poor Marianne was going to have to do a lot of work on her own. I knew she was strong and very capable, but it would be tough for her when the time of the family move came, even though I was sure that the family welfare people would look after everything.

When I left there were no flight dates set for Marianne, so there was going to be a dark period for us all. I tried to reassure her that everything would be all right, and that the Royal Marines authorities would take care of things. I was sure they would take care of their own. But in the end Marianne was badly let down by the welfare people. Seeing how things had been going on in 43 Cdo I doubt if there was even a welfare setup in place at that time.

In the meantime I had to leave them all. I flew out of Brize Norton in early March 1962. I was now beginning to feel very guilty about leaving Marianne and the family, mainly because I wasn't really happy with the welfare set up that was going to help Marianne with the move. For the first time since getting married I had no control or input in my family's safety and that did not feel good at all. I kept trying to convince myself that they would be all right and taken care of, but I wasn't happy and it took a long part of the flight to get my mind settled.

On my arrival in Singapore, I was accommodated in Nee Soon garrison with transport and composite troop. Our huts were bashas, which are like jungle huts made of bamboo with thatched roofs, no windows, very open plan. When the monsoon rain came about two o'clock every afternoon, we had to batten down the openings with pull-down shutters until the rains finished. At night the rats would run around inside the thatch roof creating all sorts of weird noises, but they never seemed to come down to ground level.

The living conditions were very basic, but we had the luxury of helpers. There were the dhobi wallas, Indian men who very professionally did our washing, starching and ironing at a very reasonable price. They had their own basha which they shared with the char walla, who made tea and egg banjos at any time of day or night. They always seemed to be available and they always knew before us when something was going to happen, such as an exercise or someone going away from the camp. If you wanted to know anything, you just asked the char walla. They also had this magic ability to pop up anywhere, in the field, on exercise or training, to keep the refreshments going.

In April I was detailed by the Commanding Officer to take ten special young men from 42 Cdo just up the road in Sembawang to carry out a special task in Aden. The task was to be two fold. The two parts involved the troopship *Devonshire* and 45 Cdo in Aden. The lads had got a weapon holdall each, with all the hardware they might need to carry out the Aden job.

We went on board as security advisors and protectors on both legs of the journey, to Aden and return. The outward journey was quite simple, as there were hardly any military personnel on board. The ship was divided into a military area and a civilian/female area. On the return journey there would be a lot more people on board of different nationalities, going from Singapore to various destinations.

It was quite a pleasant five-day cruise to Aden, not luxury, but fairly relaxed and all expenses paid. On arrival

I reported to the Intelligence Officer, who would brief me on the task. But as things turned out the task had allegedly been completed the previous day, because the situation had got too hot to leave it any longer.

That meant we had time on our hands. The lads were a bit disappointed that they weren't going to get any activity. Movement was restricted in Aden and there was no shore leave. There was not a lot to do out there.

They did have a sand golf course, with greens made from compressed sand and oil, which were rolled until very smooth. In fact they made a very reasonable putting surface. The fairways were just sand, so you carried a square of artificial turf around with you and wherever your ball landed you placed the ball on the turf and played your next shot. Most certainly it helped to take up time and was very popular.

When the time came for the *Devonshire* to return to Singapore, I went to the Intelligence Officer to get details of the civilians going on board. I asked for a passenger list, as I really wanted to know who was connected with the military and who was civilian. I was also interested in nationalities and final destinations.

I was advised by the Int Section to take a special interest in two guys who were heading for Morocco. Why were they going all the way to Singapore to get to Morocco? I detailed two of the team to watch their activities at a distance for all five days. If the two thought it wise to change the faces of the two team members, they were free to do so.

According to the passenger list there were only forty civilians and eighteen military personnel travelling. It was a totally incident-free trip, with decent weather and calm seas. The two guys travelling to Morocco kept themselves to themselves and hardly ever came out of their cabin. Perhaps they didn't like the food on board. Once we got to Singapore they were reported to the security officer in the naval base. I advised him to get them on their way to Morocco as soon as possible, without leaving them alone to disappear into downtown Singapore. The whole trip was a good learning curve for me.

Now it was back to my duties at Nee Soon Garrison. While I had been away more ranks had arrived. There was Pony Moore, the sergeant major, (not the same Pony I had known back home), Jim Vardy, the troop colour sergeant and Bernie Grivell, the clerical man, plus a number of other drivers, including my best man from Malta, Gerry Bourne. This was a great surprise and a pleasure to see him again. I could only see him during working hours because things had changed for him.

His story was that when Marianne and I left Malta in late 1959, Gerry was to follow back to England. He met up with a young lady called Betty when he was carrying out driving duties on behalf of the recruiting element of the Royal Marines which was touring the UK. He married her in 1961 and was soon after posted to Malta and on to Singapore. In Singapore he was to go home every day to Betty in Jahore Baru, where they lived in a bungalow in a Kampong Village.

In the meantime, in the very basic conditions in Nee Soon Camp, I was getting very worried about the arrival dates - or non-arrival dates - of Marianne and the family. Jim Vardy thought they would all come out together, which eased my mind a little. But apparently poor Marianne was having a rough time back home. Of course I knew nothing about this at the time, as communications were so different in those days. When the time came for the family to get the flight to Singapore there was hardly any serious procedure in hand to help.

The married quarters staff, civilians I think, came round to the house to take the hiring back. They checked the inventory and then told Marianne that she was to leave the house straight away. The flight wasn't for another 36 hours, but they made her hand the keys over and locked the house, leaving her, the little ones and the luggage on the pavement.

Thank goodness the lady across the road saw what had happened and looked after them overnight. Marianne slept on the floor, Denise slept in a sideboard drawer and Joanne in the carry cot. Poor Marianne still cries every time she talks about it. What a horrendous experience.

Now she had to get to Stansted airport, and nobody had been to see her or brief her. Luckily an SSAFA lady arrived that morning with a vehicle to take the family to Plymouth station. She gave Marianne the warrants for the train and then left. It must have been a nightmare with the two children, but at least the train journey to Paddington gave a little chance for a rest before the change of trains.

She must have felt very lonely at this point, because all the hustle and bustle was very new to her. I feel very guilty about it all even now.

She was very brave and strong and eventually got to Stansted, where she met with other wives and servicemen who were travelling to Singapore. Small mercies, a little light relief.

Now she faced the drama of a twelve-hour flight, stopping at some remote countries for refuelling. Finally at four o'clock in the morning the plane arrived, in a temperature of 100 degrees and humidity of 90. Dear Marianne came out of the lounge, in very warm clothes, with the two children, one in her arms, and all the luggage. No wonder she almost collapsed when she saw me. Denise was frightened of me because of my sun tan. It wasn't very far from the house I had rented for us all.

It took some time for Marianne to get over that experience and I hoped that she would never have to go through anything like it ever again. In this instance the corps had malfunctioned and was very sadly lacking in care and concern for my family.

For the next week or so I was able to give my full attention to the family, taking them to the naval leisure centre with a lovely swimming pool. Of course the weather was good. I had bought a car so we could travel around and see Singapore, the Raffles Hotel, the Tiger Balm gardens and all the animals.

We were at the swimming pool one day when, unbelievably, Marianne recognised her cousin Gina, last seen I believe in Malta. She was married to a Royal Marine musician in the band service here in Singapore. What a wonderful relief after the nightmare of getting to Singapore, to find a family member. They got on so very well with each other.

To top it all, I was then promoted to sergeant. This meant a lot to me. I had achieved what seemed almost impossible - to be a sergeant in the Royal Marines, after just six years and at the age of 25. The financial benefits were going to be of great help and the social life could be better if we wanted it to be.

Now in organising sporting events for my troop, I had to contact GLHQ army to try and get fixtures for soccer matches. The contact in the army turned out to be a Sergeant Collins RAOC. Collins? Could it possibly be someone I knew rather well? I was given his telephone number, so I rang his office. He answered the phone as Sergeant Collins and I replied "This is Sergeant Collins, Royal Marines. You wouldn't be Jim by any chance would you?"

"Yes" he replied.

"I appear to be your brother Tony" I said to him. I can't tell you what he said over the phone. When I explained to him that I was looking for football fixtures for our unit, he suggested that I should go up to his office in HQ to make a few fixtures.

Jim and Jean had never met Marianne and I had never met Jean, so it was going to be great for us all to get together.

The next thing I knew was that in December 1962, because of the worsening situation in Indonesia, Borneo and Brunei, we were put on standby. We just had time to fit in one football match against Jim's army team, and it was a smashing afternoon. I couldn't get the strongest team together because most of the lads were on standby or had already gone, but it was great fun, even though Jim's team were far stronger than us and they smashed us. I can't remember (or don't want to) what the score was.

As far as the world's problems were concerned, the Protectorate of Brunei was under attack from rebels at Limbang and the British resident and his wife were held hostage. In response to the trouble, various units were sent to Brunei. In the first week of December, 42 Cdo sent a company of troops and my transport and composite troop to Sabah in Sarawak. The Limbang battle was short and bloody. The hostages were released by 42 Cdo, the area was cleared in 36 hours, five lads lost their lives and seven were wounded. The confrontation with Indonesia was to go on until 1966 before there was a peace agreement.

In the meantime in Sabah, we were relatively safe. Because it was getting close to Christmas, the entertainments group, ENSA, came out to give concerts for the whole area. We also had the British Forces Broadcasting Service, which organised record requests from the families back in Singapore.

I had a lovely request from Marianne. The record was called *Mr Wonderful*, and it meant a lot to me getting that request. But you can imagine the stick I got from the lads, and of course the instigator and orchestrator was Gerry, who led the morning singsong of Sergeant Wonderful. The favourite comment was "Good morning Sergeant Wonderful", or every time they walked past me they would hum the tune.

The question on everybody's mind was - are we going to get home to Singapore in time for Christmas? With the security and safety of the area still critical, there was not a chance of us getting there quickly.

I was asked to organise a sports competition between the various units. I based it on the "It's a Knockout" TV show. There was volleyball, five-a-side soccer, five-a-side cricket and hockey. The team with the most points overall would receive medals from the Sultan of Brunei. They were big bronze medals in a blue case, unique and very collectable. A Royal Marines team won the overall points tally, and I got a medal for organising the event. Apparently it was very well enjoyed by all and took people's minds off of being away from their families.

In the early part of 1963 we were ordered back to Singapore, if I remember rightly on board HMS *Bulwark*. But the sad news was that Gerry had picked up a very bad chest infection in Borneo that wouldn't clear up. So sadly he was casevaced back to the UK. Little did I know that that was to be the last time I would see him. I didn't even get the chance to meet his wife Betty.

The whole family was sent back to the UK very promptly. It was great to see everybody at home and the family were all well and seemed to be very happy. It was a big help for Marianne to have Gina and Derek around while I was away.

Then she gave me the good news that she was pregnant again, baby due in March. I hoped that I wasn't going to be sent away anywhere for the foreseeable future.

We had some lovely parties with my brother Jim, whose wife Jean really loved parties and was the life and soul of a get together. I had a delicious party starter, a rum punch. It was a very potent, very drinkable punch, involving the contents of many different bottles, the combination of which was a fast acting and very moreish drink.

Jean always remembered one particular party at our house in Siglap on the coast road. I have never before seen a lady with such a lovely big smile on her face as she very slowly slid down the wall in our front room to the floor, where she was to stay for some time. Mind you it was the second mixing of the brew, which was probably the second ten-pint mix. It was popular with plenty of fruit salad floating around the punch bowl. We didn't meet up very often as families before Singapore, so it was nice to get together.

We were now granted a lovely bungalow hiring in Serangoon Garden Estate, a beautiful place with a long drive in a lovely clean area. We got settled into the new place, which was in very good condition, and Marianne had an ahmah (maid) to help with the chores and the children.

Jim was soon to be posted to Germany, BAOR (British Army of the Rhine). It was there that his son Jimmy became a very good footballer. He was taken on by

Münchengladbach Youth, which was at a very high level, and for German coaches to recognise and encourage an English youth player to play at that level was quite something. I was disappointed that the lad didn't pursue a soccer career, but that was his choice.

In March it was time for Marianne to go into Changi hospital to have the baby, the first time she had been in hospital, let alone given birth in one. Isobel Francis was born on Sunday 4th March 1963 in the middle of the night, so I wasn't there because I had to go home with the other girls. An early morning phone call summoned us to Changi to see Marianne and the new arrival. In those days the stay in hospital was about a week, so it meant a few journeys back and forth. Gina went a couple of times.

A couple of days later Marianne and baby came home to settle in. Now we had three girls, so I was wondering if we could we possibly have a son next...

Life did settle down for a short while. Having three lovely children ensured that life was full of activities and events, though I must say it appeared to me that they were good children.

I had a special cricket match coming up for the Royal Marines, which was to be played on the Raffles Hotel front lawn – in fact it was on the cricket pitch outside the Raffles, which was regarded as their front lawn. The game was against the Singapore select side, which included some very good Asian players, airline pilots and the like. The weather was guaranteed to be good, if the afternoon monsoon could stay away for a while. To make a day of it

I booked an evening meal in the Raffles for Marianne, Gina, Derek and myself.

The game went fine and we batted first and scored freely for the first four wickets, scoring 170 runs. Then we had a slight collapse, and ended up with a total of 245 all out.

The tea was supplied in the Raffles lounge, with plenty of ice-cold drinks. It was something special, bearing in mind the colourful history of this place.

We got off to a very good start in the field by taking their first three wickets for just 43 runs. Then their number five and the opening batsman put on 80 runs before I managed to get them both out with consecutive deliveries. I was chuffed. They went on to get 216 all out. It really was a great game played in a wonderful spirit.

The evening at the hotel was also something to remember. There was a very good resident dance band, who knew just what tunes to play. All in all a very unusual and entertaining day.

CHAPTER TEN

Back at work after the weekend, I was told by my bosses that I had been selected to take 60 of our lads to the Philippines for a special task. How I got involved in this one I don't really know. I can only assume that the unit that would normally take on this commitment, 42 Cdo, was still on standby, because the confrontation with Indonesia was still ongoing so they were better placed in Singapore.

I had about six weeks to prepare my lads for this task, with some fitness training and field work to get reasonably up to scratch. All 61 one of us were looking forward to this one, because it was going to be very different and for a short period. The American marines were going to have a big amphibious exercise off the coast of Mindare, near Passay, and they wanted very professional men to act as the enemy. I impressed upon my lads that we were representing the Royal Marines and in no way were we going to let the Corps down. "Shall we give them a hard time?" I said, and got the thumbs up with a big "Oh yes!"

The whole exercise was for just three weeks. But could we face three weeks of American food? I went to the QM and asked if we could take plenty of our own compo rations, in case the lads got a bit uppity about the American food.

We flew from Changi on a fairly short flight to Manila, where we were met by a lieutenant from the American Army. He had three coaches with him to take us to Passay, where a number of army units were temporarily based.

We were housed in very large tents. The first thing we noticed was the lack of discipline among the ranks and officers, and first names seem to be the order of the day. My first action was to get all my lads together to point out that we were not going to follow in their footsteps, and that we would maintain standards. We would have a good time, but we would show them what real soldiering was all about. By all means be friendly towards their men, I said, but above all be professional.

The food was horrible, especially breakfast, which consisted of ice-cream and pancakes - all right as a one-off novelty, but not every morning. So the first task for me was to suss out the intermediary, Lieutenant Schwarza, and ask him if my men could have an English breakfast of eggs, bacon, sausage etc, with maybe a starter of porridge or cereal and lots of bread. He asked me why, and I suggested to him that this American food tasted lovely, but would not sustain my men for the physical requirements of the forthcoming tasks. I told him the American C rations were fine and that we had of some of our compo rations if needed.

The following day I went for a briefing from the American intelligence section, and took along my two corporals with me. From the brief, what we were being asked to do sounded like a lot of fun. As their troops were landing, some fireworks had been arranged by the American army. We were to ensure that we were watching them from a short distance, and if we wanted to, let them know that we were there, but we were to ensure that no one got captured. We were to travel away from the beachhead and select our own route, making sure that we climbed to high ground so that we pushed them to their limits. The exercise was going to last about 72 hours, on the move practically all the time. The start was at 055hrs in three days' time, so the boys had time to go to the NAAFI (PX) to see what was on offer; they could buy items after the exercise was over. It was no good leaving the presents they had bought for loved ones in an open tent.

As requested, there was a change of breakfast the following morning and it was appreciated by the boys. I thanked the chefs and found Lieutenant Schwarza and thanked him very much on behalf of my lads. He seemed surprised to get any thanks - maybe that was the difference in nationalities.

I got the impression that some of the American soldiers liked the smell of the English breakfast and took a fancy to it. The chefs would call out "sunny side up or down?" to my boys, who learned very quickly what it meant.

The next day I took a recce party of about a dozen towards the beach, to get some idea of the terrain. I also sent my two corporals in the opposite direction down the mountainside to see the route we would return by if we needed a good escape route.

That evening we all went across to the PX bar for an evening get-together and a couple of drinks. We all got on very well with the Americans, with lots of laughter and jokes. One particular American had had too many drinks and was shouting off to the point where he was becoming abusive and insulting. This was upsetting one or two of my boys, who stood up, quite prepared to take action if required. I could see that the situation could turn nasty, so I went across to the individual concerned and asked him to tone down his attitude. At the same time a sergeant from the American army came across. At first I thought he was going to tackle me about the situation, but he was there to back me up and have the individual removed from the building. It all calmed down after that, and I invited him across to have a drink with us all. It was a good way for a trouble hotspot to end. My words to the boys about no trouble paid off. These Americans in this area were not assault troops but the administrative and quartermaster group.

I told the boys to get a good night's sleep the night before the landing. That morning we were up, washed and dressed by 0330hrs, our packs ready with enough emergency clothing for two days and plenty of water. Our pouches were packed with thunderflashes and blanks. We had a good early breakfast and selected our ration packs for three days, so foodwise we were ready. Off we went to await dawn.

From the high ground we could see everything. The Americans had covered the beach with explosive devices, all along the beachhead, as they had said they would. These were to be set off electronically.

At dawn we could see the assault ships heading for the beach, about ten craft in all, so we estimated that about 200 marines were going to land.

On the beach the devices were let off and the American marines were spread out along the beachhead. They were kept down for a while. They would have to start climbing, which gave us the chance to let them have a few nasties before retreating a little. But now they knew we were there. I had split my lads into two groups, one on each flank so we would not be overrun. We would let off a few rounds every so often so that the Americans didn't lose us. We kept pretty much on the move at a brisk pace, but not so fast that we left them far behind. After all we were playing games with them.

Once they got over the high ground the terrain flattened out a bit, so we had to make sure we were on the next area of high ground. After about four hours on the move, we could see that they were having a rest. So we pushed higher for about an hour, to give us time on our hands to rustle up some scran.

They now had to start hunting for us, and we didn't leave them lots of clues because out training was against that. We decided to make a couple of false trails, just to keep them interested. We even thought about making some bows and arrows and firing thunder flashes through the air, but decided against it in case it all went wrong and someone got injured. So we relied on craft to maintain the gap between us. We laid a couple of false trails off to the left, some English compo litter spread here and there.

As soon as they stopped and bedded down for the night, we would push on for another hour before stopping and resting. We thought we were always too far in front for any patrols to ping us. We had a system of guard duties on our fringes which were more like mobile patrols. I thought they might send out some patrols, so we needed to ping them early. I told my guys to be very alert and if they thought that they heard anything then not to be afraid to give us the alert so we could be on the move, even if there was no one around.

We had a decent night's rest and were very alert at dawn. We could see that they had taken our false trail off to the left, so that gave us time for a bit of breakfast before moving.

I don't know if the Americans had been instructed specifically to seek out and capture us, because they were using search tactics rather than an assault landing approach. Every so often they would send out a group as far as half a mile ahead of the remainder, so when that happened, we would make a false trail even further to the left flank. All the time they were taking a trail it would take them further away to the left and away from us, which gave us more breathing space, but it also meant we couldn't lay down any fire on them. But as long as they were using search tactics we had to make sure we stayed one step ahead of them.

At the suggestion of the boys, we decided that the next day, the last day of the exercise, we would lay a trail in the afternoon to bring them close to us, at the base of a very steep hill. Then we would lay an ambush as they climbed the hill. We would get rid of all our remaining thunderflashes and ammunition from directly above them, then escape along the route pre-planned by my JNCOs as our escape route back to camp.

That night we stopped near what appeared to be a jungle village. We could see the locals a little distance away but we didn't want to get involved or intrude in case they had poison darts and wanted some practice. I didn't know the political situation with the indigenous people, so I thought it wise to avoid them.

Early the following morning, we could hear the Americans over to our left. We could also smell their cigarettes and aftershave, smells which travelled a long way in those hills.

We set off after breakfast leaving a refuse pit of our rubbish, uncovered as though we had forgotten to fill it in. The Americans must have thought they were closing in on us, because they were moving quite fast. We had the advantage of being above them all the time, and come lunchtime we climbed higher and set the ambush. I sent Corporal Jackson plus two others forward to check that we were on our escape route.

When he came back he reported that one of the boys had twisted his ankle and was in a lot of pain. The medic checked him out, strapped his ankle up and suggested that we send him back, to make his own way at his own pace. I sent Corporal Jackson and six marines with him in case he had to be carried. The rest of us had our lunch and prepared our reception for the Americans. We could see they were just approaching the base of the very steep hill, and as they came across the open ground we moved slightly higher, just to make sure we couldn't be caught.

Five hundred feet below us the Americans were just starting to climb. We threw all our remaining nasties at them and the thunderflashes went off above their heads. This kept their heads down for some time and we made our escape back to base.

Now something happened which really made us laugh. As we worked our way up the final part of the tree-covered hill and came out into the open, we saw in front of us a number of refrigerated vehicles and above them a sign which read "The 43rd American Ice Cream Unit". What a laugh. No wonder they had it for breakfast, lunch and dinner!

As we got near the base camp I got the boys fell in in three ranks, then marched them to our tents and halted them. I impressed upon the lads that I was going to report to Lieutenant Schwarza and get his permission to stand down. I informed him that the assault troops were at the base of the hill to our right. I did ask him if he wanted to speak to the lads, but I think that was all a bit new for him. He gave permission to end the exercise for my lads, so they could now go and get a much-needed shower and shave. I thanked them for the brilliant job they had done and gave them a couple of days off for rest and recuperation. They didn't need telling to get their dhobi done and get up to date.

We were due to fly out the following Sunday from Manila. While I was in the Philippines I asked an American sergeant if they still had cowboy silver dollars and he told me there were a few around, but they were getting rarer. He kindly said he would ask the PX manager if he had any or could get any. Later that day he came back with an 1889 silver dollar, big and heavy. He let me buy it off him at the face value of one new dollar, which was good of him. I still have it today, almost fifty years on.

It was now time to go home to Singapore, so Lieutenant Schwarza organised the buses to Manila and we were on our way. I think the boys really did enjoy the trip, because it was not too stressful or strenuous and not too long.

The flight was great, because we were heading in the right direction. Transport was waiting for us at Changi. It was lovely to be home with the family, and I think they were pleased to see me. I hope so anyway. Maybe I was going to get a little stability at home, and it was good that I would start off by being there for Christmas.

Back at work in Nee Soon after a few days' leave, there didn't appear to be anything on the horizon that would take us away. My fingers were crossed.

The Royal Singapore Golf Club had recently opened on the Bukit Timar road. It was a cracking course, so I decided to have a go at it. I had never played serious golf before, as you could hardly call the Aden venture serious golf. First I went to the range, which was packed with new golfers. It was a very well-organised range, especially the ball collectors. They weren't mechanical, but human. Ladies with big umbrellas walked down the length of the

Expecting our first child,
Exmouth, Devon 1960

Jim's wife Jean

My brother Jim, at work for a change

Derek, Gina, Marianne and AC enjoying a night out in the
Raffles Hotel, Singapore

My brother Jim's son Jimmy,
a very good footballer

The Collins kids, now grown up

Far East champions, FA Army Cup 1961: brother Jim's team in
Singapore doing what he does best, winning trophies.

1965 - I show my respect to Lord Mountbatten as
he arrives at Earl's Court, Royal Box

Royal Tournament 1965. On security duty to protect
Princess Alexandra in the Royal Box

With our new-born son Marc in Deal, Kent,1966

1967-8 - the day RM Deal Kent played
against Kent Seconds with Derek Underwood

1972 - presentation of long service and good conduct medals
by the CO of Eastney Barracks

1972 - presentation of LSGC Medal

This unique dance area, where many servicemen spent a lot of time.
'THE CHALET'

range with their backs towards the golfers. They picked up the balls in plastic tubes and put them into large bags slung over their shoulders. They were very brave and skilful and kept the range pretty clear of golf balls. One way to earn a living I suppose. No one seemed to get injured. I have not seen that system anywhere else in the world - health and safety I suppose. From the range I eventually progressed to playing a round of golf on the course proper, by which time I suppose you could say I was hooked.

I'm not sure if Marianne was too happy that I had taken up a new sport, but I didn't play very much, as even out here it was very expensive. But before I left I got my first set of golf clubs, which were second-hand and reasonably priced. I don't think I used them on the golf course out here. Knowing I would be going back to the UK in the near future, I packed them in our household boxes for when it was time to get ready.

We in the UK could learn an awful lot from the Singaporeans about giving a good service to the general public. The local shopkeepers were masters at public relations. They were so polite and helpful, whether you wanted to buy anything or not, and worked tirelessly day or night to make a living. For example, when I went for a haircut, the shop would have five or six chairs and the same number of cutters waiting to serve you. The first thing you were asked was if you would like a cold drink. Then you would get a complete head massage, which lasted a couple of minutes, followed by a hot flannel facewash which would also last a couple of minutes. Then the haircut itself, to your instructions, followed by a shoulder massage before you got out of the chair, a luxurious experience and all for two Singapore dollars, about two shillings at that time.

We spent Christmas and New Year as a family group; I can't even remember if there was a sergeant's mess function. I do remember the first Singapore Grand Prix, which was for racing motor cycles in those days. Riders from all over the world came, along with local riders and some military riders. It was a new event, with a course built around Nee Soon and the embankment road heading into town. Of course all the streets in the area were closed, so it was a day off for anyone who worked in the naval base, Sembawang and Nee Soon. It was a very exciting event, but far too noisy for the girls.

As a proud father, one of most lovely things I could do, which gave me enormous pleasure, was dressing them in beautiful clothes whenever you took them out. Most of the time the girls wore just swimming trunks, so it was great to dress them up occasionally. The local markets were full of very good children's clothes.

We were now into 1964 and there was very little military activity, so it was just the daily routine at work, with more opportunities to have fun with the family. Marianne and I decided to take them up to a wonderful beach in Malaya for a few days to picnic and swim. Marianne prepared a lot of wonderful food, including a roast chicken. The place we were going to was a cove near Malacca, so it was a fair drive, but we had been told it was like the beaches in the Hawaiian islands.

It was a lovely morning when we set off, and the girls were very excited. Marianne was pleased to have a day out and to see Malaya. We drove across the causeway into Jahore Bahru, following the Kuala Lumpur road. The scenery had changed to the rubber plantations, so we stopped for a few minutes to watch a planter tapping the trees for rubber sap. He cut a groove around the tree and where the groove ended, he had a tin tied to the tree and the rubber ran down the groove into the tin. I suppose he would have to empty the tins quite frequently so the rubber didn't overflow.

About half an hour later we arrived at the bay. It was beautiful and deserted and the sea looked very calm, clear and blue. I laid out a couple of blankets and we settled the children, who were dying to get into the water. While I was getting the food from the car and laying it out on the blanket, Marianne took the children to the water's edge. It was a smashing scene, so I decided to join them in the water. What we didn't know was that a local dog must have been lurking in the bushes just off to our right, because no sooner had I got to the family in the water than this beast was running away to our right with our roast chicken in its mouth, gone forever. It was annoying, but very funny. We had plenty of other food, but from that moment on the area was never left unguarded. Apart from that incident it was a smashing day out, dozing and having fun all day until quite late.

The next few months were relatively quiet, with nothing more than the odd exercise up country for a couple of days at a time. We began to plan our move back to the UK, now only a few months away. I learned that we were going to Deal in Kent; once again a full circle since joining the Royal Marines. Gina and Derek were also being posted to Deal, Derek to join the RM School of Music as an instructor.

I had the idea of asking the Military Movements Office if our flights back to the UK could be via Malta, on a semi-compassionate basis. If this was approved it would be a wonderful surprise for Marianne, at least I hoped so. Her parents could see their lovely grandchildren for the first time, so I was hoping the Movements Office would be sympathetic.

To my surprise and delight, our request was accepted. I rushed home that afternoon to give the family the good news. Marianne could see from the big smile on my face that something was going on. I told her to sit down, then said we were going to spend nearly all our repatriation leave in Malta. We would fly from Singapore to Malta and then on to the UK after our leave.

"What do you think of that?" I said. She said she couldn't believe it, and the tears were flowing. I said I would find out the timing as soon as they were known and then she could send a letter to her parents with the news.

In the meantime we had to get busy packing our repatriation boxes with all the household possessions we had accumulated over the past three years. These boxes would be shipped to the UK well in advance of our leaving, and they would, we hoped, be in Deal when we arrived, having completed our leave in Malta.

Finally the details came through. We were flying out of Singapore on or about the 27th September by RAF Trident to Tripoli, where the aircraft would refuel and go on to the UK, leaving the Collins family for an ongoing flight across the Med to Malta. After three weeks of leave there we would be flown by the RAF to Brize Norton. All details had been arranged by Movements in Singapore. This was all brilliant from Marianne's point of view, as there was no repetition of the inward journey.

On my next day at work I went to the movements office to thank them for all their efforts. They told me my relief was arriving the next day, a Sergeant Thomas. I was to spend the next couple of weeks handing everything over to him. I think I even sold my car to him. At a knockdown price, of course!

CHAPTER ELEVEN

The day arrived when we were due to fly out of Singapore for the last time, this time travelling as a family. An RAF Trident was waiting on the tarmac to take us to Tripoli. The flight was comfortable and we were very well looked after by the RAF in-flight staff. I think every member of the family was getting a little excited, but it was necessary for us to get some rest. The children were all very good on the flight, entertaining themselves with books and drawings and the occasional sleep. I fell asleep going back over my adventures and experiences in Singapore over the past few years.

When we arrived at Tripoli, I was informed that the next flight across the water was a Dakota which was empty, but there were no seats because it was a cargo run. They said they would put in four seats for us, or we could wait an unknown amount of days for the next flight, which could be the same as this one. So I thought we might as well get going straight away and get it over with. I told Marianne, and we decided to take the plane.

The craft really was a banger. The doors had huge gaps around them, so I hoped we weren't going to fly too high. It was also very cold and noisy. At one point I thought we were going to be issued with parachutes. There was only the pilot and one other crew on board, so I assumed that there wasn't going to be any on board catering! I did not dare not ask where the toilets were. But then it was only going to be a maximum of one hour across the water, so it didn't really matter.

No one in Malta knew at what time we were going to arrive because we didn't know ourselves. So when we touched down with a bump at RAF Luqa, there were no customs awaiting us and I don't think anybody knew we were on board.

I thanked the pilot for the lift and jokingly said to him, "I'll see you in three weeks when you take us back to Brize Norton". He laughed and said "I'll try and get this machine for you."

We took a taxi from Luqa to Marianne's parents' place. I remember the taxi driver really struggling to get the five big suitcases in the boot - he had to stack them and rope them. I was very pleased I had labelled every suitcase with the address, because one of them dropped off on the bumpy roads. Another motorist following behind the taxi picked the suitcase up and kindly followed us to the address on the label, in Gzira. Thank goodness.

What an exciting moment to see the happiness on the faces of the family. They hadn't seen Marianne for five years and now she had three lovely children. Before long, sisters and brothers were appearing from all over the island. It was a lovely get together and a lovely moment.

The children were so very young that they didn't really

know what was going on. It was all a bit bewildering for them, being squeezed and cuddled endlessly. They were also pretty exhausted - they had managed hardly any sleep in the last 24 hours - but they weren't miserable about it.

This was a very emotional time for the adults and I thought it best if I tried to slow the situation down a little and try to get everybody to relax and enjoy the moments. A good night's sleep was required for a fresh start tomorrow.

On waking up I found the children still asleep, which was a big surprise, because normally they would be romping around the house. They must have been in need of a very good sleep.

It was going to be a nice day, so maybe we would spend some time relaxing by the sea. I knew we would be expected to go around to all the aunties and uncles, but I felt a day of rest would be better for us all. A day at St George's Bay might be a good idea.

I hired a car from the relative with the garage, which would allow us to get around a bit. But first I wanted to get confirmation from RAF Luqa about our return flight details, so we could relax and enjoy the leave period.

We were now in 1965, and many things had come full circle. Perhaps we should visit Imtarfa, Grand Harbour, St Andrews and St George's barracks and maybe even have a day out at Ghajn Tuffieha beach. Much of this was personal to me, but it would also be nice for the others. Returning to Malta seemed to have made half my life flash before me.

I was expecting Marianne's sister Rose to arrive at the house very soon after breakfast, and sure enough she turned up. It was time to continue with the enjoyment of this family reunion in this lovely little country, with lovely people. We had to make the most of it, because we didn't know when, if ever, another opportunity would come.

Malta was full of wonderful memories of some of the happiest times of my life, those times as a young man when happiness is important and your life is being influenced by the good around you. I found that high quality peers make high quality people, and trash makes trash. Malta is full of high quality people.

We spent the next couple of weeks letting Marianne enjoy the closeness of her family around her. We had a lovely time on holiday, with lots of love and smiles. But it was soon time to travel back to the UK to continue our lives as a family, a military family to boot. Because we had spent most of our leave in Malta, we only had one week to get settled into our new role.

We arrived at Brize Norton not in the Dakota, but in a Trident, thank goodness. There was a train journey across to London, then on to the South Kent, and another full circle was complete.

We had been allocated a married quarter in Trafalgar Square Barracks and settled in fairly quickly. Denise would soon be going to school and perhaps Joanne would go to prep school.

I was now in the transport department at Deal. This was where they had taken our kitbags from to Lympstone, when I was a recruit. Deal barracks was one of the better barracks, very kind on the eye once you got to know the whole place. Although it was a very old established barracks, it had loads of character.

The sergeants' mess was open to me as a sergeant and it overlooked the main gates, which were all part of the front lawn. This included the lovely cricket pitch, which was also overlooked by the officers' mess.

I was to play a lot of cricket on this pitch, because as a training establishment the pace of life was much slower than at a commando unit. There were many more social functions, with a lot more time for parent-child relations.

Soon after arriving at Deal , we decided that the time was right for us to get on the property ladder. We found a nice house just round the corner from our married quarter in Forelands Square. In fact we found that Gina and Derek had already got a place further round the square. Having the responsibility of a mortgage meant that finances were tighter, but that was not as important as getting on to the housing ladder.

I had much more stability at work now and was able to carry out a lot of work on the house. We loved the place, it was ours and the children were very happy there.

Of course life wasn't always carefree. One day Marianne called me in a panic to say that Isobel, who was still only two, had disappeared. I thought that if I walked from my office back towards our house I would come across her, if she had come that way. I got all the way home and there was no sign of her, but just as I got to the front door a man rolled up on a pushbike with Isobel sitting in the wicker basket on his handlebars. She was loving every minute of it. It seemed she had decided to go for a walk, out of the back garden and off down the road, apparently to look for her dad. She managed to get a mile from home, and how she did it we will never know.

I asked him how he had found us, and he said Isobel had just got to the barracks when he saw her. He stopped and asked her where she was going and she said "Daddy" and pointed to the barracks. The man knew the marines lived in Trafalgar and Foreland Squares, so he put her in the basket and toured around looking for a parent in distress. Marianne had appeared, crying her eyes out, so very relieved to see Isobel safe.

That situation was really frightening and we never wanted it to happen again. The one thing that can be said at that time was that there was no concern about paedophilia, only about a child being hurt.

Many servicemen were commenting on the financial constraints that were beginning to bite around 1965. Many more people had bought property and cars and were feeling the pinch. I took on an extra job in the Dover docks evenings and weekends, unloading ships by hand - all sorts of things, timber, bananas and crated goods. It was kept very quiet in the barracks, because there were a lot of people who felt the need to earn extra money. I think a blind eye was turned by the senior officers, because they knew the financial situation in the country was making it very difficult for everybody. We were all trying to protect our families from poverty.

I knew Marianne was now carrying our fourth child, so that made me more determined to do what was right for the family. If we needed some extra cash I would go to the dockyard gates early on a Saturday morning and hope that I was taken on for the day, to be given cash in hand at the end of the shift. If necessary the same would happen on Sunday morning. We never knew if there was going to be any work, but when there was, it all helped to buy food and to pay for the decorating inside and outside the house.

In June 1966, World Cup year, I was in Canterbury, due to play cricket for the Royal Marines, when a message came through on the "dog and bone" to tell me to get home quickly as the baby was on its way. I set off immediately. On getting home I rushed through the front door and was about to run upstairs, but on the stairs appeared Marianne's best friend, who appeared to be deliberately blocking me from getting up the stairs. She started telling me what had gone on. The delay was deliberate - how could she do this to Marianne? I remember all this because at a later date I would be reminded that I had spent time talking to this woman at the bottom of the stairs instead of going straight up to see my wife. But that couldn't have been further from the truth. I was getting used to these accusations.

Anyway that didn't prevent this from being a wonderful day, because I soon discovered that our marvellous first son had arrived. We called him Marc, and I think I could now say that our family was complete.

The time we spent at Deal was good, and my work

was really very easy, it didn't involve going away much, and it was quite simple to administer and maintain a fleet of vehicles.

One day my commanding officer was approached to supply personal protection to the Royal Family in the Royal Box at the Royal Tournament at Earls Court in London. Four SNCOs including myself were nominated to attend. It was for only two weeks and we could come home at weekends. It was great to be so close to Her Majesty, Prince Philip, a staunch Royal Marines man, Lord Louis Mountbatten, another Royal Marines man and a number of the princesses and other members of the Royal Family. We were used as a close protection party, unarmed. The social life at Deal was very good with many sporting activities.

As a matter of interest Colour Sergeant Tyack was back from Malta and once again ensconced at Deal. His wife got on very well with Marianne at the sergeants' mess functions and cricket matches, because Roger, as I could now call him, played cricket with me in the unit team.

I was beginning to have a few regrets about becoming a tradesman instead of staying on general duties, because since leaving Singapore I had not been a real Commando, but I suppose that was a result of promotions and being posted to training establishments. Life was so much slower and less active.

Let me tell you about a particular game of cricket we had on the front pitch against Kent seconds. It was a charity game and the public could walk in and enjoy the game and contribute to the cause if they wanted to. We knew the Kent team would be too strong for us, but we were determined to give it a hundred per cent. Included in the Kent side were Colin Cowdrey's son and Derek Underwood, the England spin bowler, who was a classic player.

I was the unit captain for this particular game, which was a great honour for me. Although I was a competitive player and a very fast bowler, I felt it important to ask the lads to enjoy the game, not to worry about the result, and enjoy the presence of these wonderful players.

We thought it best that Kent should bat first to enable the public to see these good players perform. They batted for two and a half hours and scored almost 250 runs for six wickets.

Tea was taken in the sergeants' mess, with delicious sandwiches and cakes, and both teams enjoyed the surroundings. After tea it was our turn to bat, and we did have one or two good batsmen. Their pace bowlers only bowled at half pace - I think they would have killed us bowling flat out. We got to 104 for four, and when I had to go in Derek Underwood came on to bowl. Whether it was out of sympathy for me or not I don't know, but at least he bowled at a pace I could see. But he had a plan up his sleeve. The umpire had an orange in his pocket. First Derek bowled a couple of very slow loopers which I managed to hit for runs. The third ball was the orange, which I swung at and of course it splattered all over the place, no runs. The next ball was a genuine ball which turned me inside out but missed the stumps – just.

I went on to score fifteen, then he bamboozled me with one which I just nicked to the wicket keeper, who appealed, but I was already walking - the umpire, Bernie Grivell, had not heard it. The team went on to score 170 runs before they were all out.

Both teams walked round the ground thanking the public and then went in to the mess for a nice cold drink and a short get-together. Normally the sergeants' mess would have an evening function for the wives to attend, but on this occasion the Kent side had already declined because they had a real game at Canterbury the following day. It was a great day, one of many we held at Deal.

There were rugby matches on the great rugby pitches in the barracks and the unit had a very good soccer team - one or two of the RM Band members were good enough to play for Dover and Folkestone. We also had a lot of good golfers and two magnificent golf courses in Deal, Kingsdown Golf Club and The Royal Cinque Ports Golf Club, while just up the road at Sandwich was the Princes Golf Club. Both the latter courses were of British Open standard and were high-quality links courses, very difficult to play if the weather was against you. But it was great fun and an experience to play these courses.

They both had artisan members for the working-class people of the area, and the caddies, ground staff and HM Forces were artisans. The Royal Marines had a fixture against the Royal Cinque Ports and Kent Golf Clubs which went on for forty years until 2005, when overseas commitments prevented us from fielding a quality team to match their standard. Too many ex-royals were being called in to play, and some of them were good golfers, others not so good. I played in my last match, with my grandson as my caddie, when I was 68 years old. I suppose you could say that was why we couldn't match their standard!

Back to the story. In 1967 my boss, Colour Sergeant Garland, was deliberating about retiring from the forces and taking his family to Australia to start a new life. It appeared he was pretty set on the idea. He retired later that year with the full intention of moving abroad, and I never saw or heard of him after that.

I was promoted to Colour Sergeant myself at the start of the New Year, 1978. As a result of this, the family finances were much improved. Because I had been promoted rather quickly and was qualified for promotion to sergeant major, it was suggested that I attend the advance command course at Lympstone. This was only a two-week course to get up to scratch in parade work and military law, which all sergeant majors need to know about, because they need to advise officers on such matters. As it was such a short course I was back home in no time.

I could see that there was going to be a move for me in the not-too-distant future. While on the course, I had words with the promotions Warrant Officer, who hinted that I was in line for a move to Portsmouth as the warrant officer to take over the driver training school in the role of what the army call Master Driver. I warned Marianne about the likely move, which would take place in about a year's time. In the meantime we had to continue with our very mundane but stable life, and in retrospect it was a good life. The children were all growing up very rapidly, enjoying their schooldays for Denise and Joanne with Isobel about to start.

We put the house on the market, much to my regret now, because in retrospect I realise it was the wrong decision for those times. I should have hung on to it until we had found a place to purchase in Portsmouth. By selling before repurchasing we fell out of the market, because property values rose much too fast to keep up with. The house sold very quickly to a friend and we stayed in it until my move was upon us.

Although we had been very stable for the past five years, it was now time to move on. I was promoted to warrant officer with the expected move to Portsmouth. I was told I was the youngest warrant officer in the Corps, which made me very proud.

We were going from one training establishment to another. Being in a training establishment was very different from being in a commando unit. The hustle and bustle of commando life was missing, and military life was more regimental. It had to be that way for the sake of maintaining standards, while individuals were learning to do other things. For example, vehicle mechanics, drivers, signallers and armourers all had to be trained while maintaining their regimental disciplines.

So we as a family moved to Portsmouth and were given

a lovely old house right on the beach on the far side of Eastney barracks. We could sit in the old boathouse at the bottom of our garden and look out over the beach and the sea. It was a smashing family home, especially for the children, with a nice big garden, the beach and sea on one side and the sports pitches on the other side.

Unfortunately we could not find a suitable house to buy, because people were becoming wise and hanging on to what they already owned. Prices were rising far too quickly, so we were out. At least we had nice accommodation, so the pain was easier to bear.

My office was in the technical training wing in Fort Cumberland, a very old fort with a long history about it. At the time I took over driver training, new heavy goods vehicle laws had just been brought in, so there were lots of changes to be made in driving instruction and it was an interesting period for a new comer to introduce his own methods.

All my instructors had to go away to get qualified as HGV examiners, a qualification which was obtained at Harmondsworth, London and had to be carried out over a long period of time so that normal training could continue and the flow of drivers needed to maintain our unit strengths would not be disrupted. All the upper management of the school had to be qualified, and in my view better qualified than the instructors. Senior ranks, including myself, went to the Metropolitan Police Driving Academy at Hendon to qualify as advanced skilled drivers, which included high-speed chases, very skilled skidpan driving and control and a very detailed knowledge of the Highway Code and transport law. A pass mark of 95 per cent was the benchmark.

Bearing in mind that with the introduction of HGV licences we could not retest every driver in the British Forces, most of the existing qualified drivers had their licences converted to HGV, but even that involved a lot of administration.

Slowly but surely the new system was enforced and the RM driving school was almost the first establishment to get up and running with qualified personnel. We had to start training not only military personnel but the fire service as well, because all their main vehicles were heavy goods and they would need examiners to keep their numbers up to date. The same applied to the police and the Royal Navy, who could all then go on to instruct and examine their own staff. Overall it was a very long programme which took a couple of years to fully fulfil all the legal requirements. It was a very busy and rewarding time for me at work, but there was always time for play, social or sporting.

I must tell you about my encounter with Geoff Capes, the champion strong man and shot putter. In around June 1970, he and Bill Tancred were training on the sports pitches outside our house. They were preparing, I believe for the Commonwealth Games, or maybe the Olympics. Geoff was a policeman and became world famous on television, and Bill was in the navy and a discus thrower. They spent a number of days out there training. At the weekend they were invited to a sergeants' mess function. Bill I think was married and went home for the weekend, but Geoff came to the function in the evening.

Marianne and I attended with a number of my instructors and their ladies. The evening went along nicely with plenty of drinks flowing. The music was playing in the background, not too loudly to stop you holding a conversation, and people were dancing. Geoff Capes came across and joined us at our table, and being a policeman he was a good talker. He asked me if he could dance with Marianne. Looking at the size of him I was hardly going to say no, was I? But I couldn't see it working, Geoff being six foot five and 23 stone and Marianne five foot two and weighing not much more than one of his shot putts.

Anyway off they went, and from start to finish I don't think Marianne's feet touched the floor once. Everyone could see the funny side of it. It was hilarious, but it was nice for Geoff holding Marianne so close! It was a very good function with lots of fun.

The cricket pitch at Eastney was used for most top games. It was a wonderful ground in a beautiful setting, with the old pavilion tucked away in the corner, and the cathedral-like barrack church directly behind the green grass of the pitch.

One day I had a big game for the Corps against the Royal Engineers, a regular fixture with a lot of rivalry. We started at eleven, and Derek Oakley was our captain for the day. I hadn't seen him since the Suez campaign. We won the toss and Derek decided to put the other side in.

Marianne said she would come over with the children after lunch, which was good because I would be in the field bowling or fielding, for the morning anyway.

At lunchtime it was a sit-down meal, a salad for the players supplied by the main galley staff. Then back to the field. By 2.15 they were 210 for eight and shortly after all out for 243.

We had a good opening partnership and put on 140 before losing a wicket. Marianne and the children, all beautifully dressed, came across the soccer pitches from home, so I went to meet them and ushered them all around the ground to some seats near the pavilion. If the children got bored they could go and play ball on the soccer pitches.

At teatime everybody came off the pitch. I was due to bat at number 6, so I got my pads on. We were now 180 for 3, so I was next in. There were a lot of spectators around the pavilion. As the next wicket fell I got up, picked up my bat and started to walk to the wicket, when Marianne called to me "don't be long, will you!" I turned back and smiled, and said "OK". The spectators were clapping and laughing, and dear Marianne didn't know why. Later she asked me why were had been clapping me and I said they had been clapping her for telling me not to be long. Of course I was supposed to stay out there as long as possible to win the game.

As it turned out I didn't need to be out there too long as we only needed 30 runs to win. It was not my style, but I had to stay there because the opening batsman was still approaching his century. I wasn't going to do anything silly at that stage. He went on to score 110 and I stayed long enough to get 20, both of us not out.

After the game, beer was served from the pavilion bar and everyone hung around for a couple of hours. I had a kick around with the gang and then walked home across the fields.

I remember a game at Poole in Dorset. I was living at Deal, the start was 11.30 and I had to drive 260 miles, leaving home at 3.30 am. I knew this was going to be a silly day. I arrived on the green at Poole harbour at 10.30 and although I was fit and strong, age was beginning to creep up on me. To drive over 200 miles to play a game of cricket, then drive back home again, was a bit over the top. But I was committed to that game and completed it. Mind you, I made my excuses about going for a drink afterwards. I had to be very careful when driving home that night, as I knew I would be tired. In those days there were no motorways along the south coast, it was all A and B class roads. At least there wasn't as much traffic then.

I got home at three in the morning, creeping indoors to try not to wake anybody, but Marianne was waiting up for me.

The next period of my career was a bit chaotic. Because of the military cuts that were going on, Eastney barracks was going to be closed with Deal barracks. Both in due course were sold to developers and are now very luxurious property complexes. They are lovely flats keeping the old façade.

With Eastney closing the driving school and technical training had to move to Poole in Dorset, which meant a lot of work for me and my team surveying Dorset for new training routes. The move went ahead and was just completed before I was posted back to 42 Cdo as Sergeant Major, a full circle was completed. I went off to Northern Ireland for a six-month tour with my transport lads, who were spread all over Belfast. They were patrolling the streets in Macralan-protected Land Rovers day and night.

I was based in an old Cyril Lord carpet factory with HQ company. Every day or so I would go out in an unmarked car with an escort, to speak to my lads who were living in atrocious conditions, getting very little sleep. I had to have words with some of the other sergeant majors about overloading the drivers by putting them on guard duties as well as their driving duties. I said they could not do both and maintain safety. Driving was their priority.

One day when I was the duty officer at the factory, I was doing my rounds when I discovered that a certain SNCO was missing from the base. I ordered a search of the area and carried out an investigation to find out whether he was officially out of the base on a duty run somewhere. The main gate security had not booked him out. At this point I had no option but to report him as missing.

Soon afterwards, a message came over the radio that a dead body had been discovered by the police about a mile from our base. Of course we all feared the worse. As it turned out it wasn't our man, because he came back to the base the same way he had left, through a side exit, without letting anybody know. He had been on an unofficial social run. I had to place him on open arrest and at his court martial he was demoted. At least that was better than being the corpse found down the road.

It was now 1973 and I was coming towards the end of my military career with just five years left to serve. While I was in Northern Ireland I learned from brother Jim that Dad had passed away at 64 years of age with a heart attack. Jim was in London with him at the time, having just left the army. Our stepmother was still in the house, now on her own because her daughter had died of cancer. But Jim, now working in London, was able to keep an eye on her. A sort of role reversal.

CHAPTER TWELVE

Out of the blue I received some wonderful news - we were being posted to Malta for the last four years or so of my time, to take over 41 Cdo transport troop of 100 men and vehicles. This was a brilliant-end-of career posting, and it really couldn't have been better if I had written the script myself.

Back at Bickleigh Camp, which had now been totally rebuilt and was a first-class barracks. It was ideal to house a commando unit, with a new sergeants' mess with lots of hot water everywhere! But outside the main gate was still the dreaded Heartbreak Hill. It was always going to be there, and rightly so.

Our overseas boxes were packed and shipped to Malta in no time. We were all very excited about the move. I knew 41 Cdo was being moved around a lot, but being sited in the Mediterranean was a critical position with the Middle East and Cyprus troubles. At least I would know that the family couldn't be better placed if I had to leave them.

Flight day at Brize Norton was a familiar routine and a lot less hassle than many of the trips in the past. Transport was waiting for us at Luqa airport and the driver was able to tell us that we had been allocated a married quarter in St Andrews barracks, alongside the gymnasium and tennis courts. It was a smashing house, like a castle, with a balcony and flat roof space, all overlooking the parade ground. We could walk down the hill to St George's barracks. Another full circle had been completed, from getting my first stripe to heading for the end of my career as a Warrant Officer.

My workplace and office were on the far side of the barracks. The children's schools were military schools, the girls went by bus and Marc's school was in the barracks, so he could walk across the parade ground to his school.

Marianne of course had a lovely reunion with the family and would meet up with everyone quite frequently, naturally.

Having just arrived and got settled in, I was told to prepare for a rapid move with my MT Troop to Cyprus to cover the Spearhead move of 40 Cdo RM, which had been flown from the UK to Cyprus to stop the Turkish invasion of the island in its tracks. At risk were the Sovereign Bases and the British residence. We were tasked to evacuate the residence from the grip of the Turkish forces.

We boarded HMS Albion with nearly all of our vehicles on or about the 20th July 1974 and in no time at all found ourselves in Famagusta. 40 Commando's prompt arrival in Cyprus had prevented the Turkish forces from moving very far from their landing point at Nicosia and Kyrenia. I was tasked to get round to Kyrenia and Pathos where there were a large number of British residence and other Nationals.

As I said, the Turkish Army had got as far as Kyrenia but were prevented by 40 Cdo from getting any closer to the British Sovereign bases, which were well protected, and it appeared that the Turkish Army were not too keen to take on the Royal Marine Commandos. They had made their point about the partition of Cyprus.

It was their intent to grab as much land and property as they could to try and equal the balance between the rich Greek areas and the poor Turkish areas. It is my belief that 40 Cdo and ourselves could have very easily driven the Turkish forces off the island had we been given the go ahead. But politically it was a Cyprus/Turkey problem and the outcome was going to be decided by the two governments, without a shot being fired as far as I know. In the meantime we had put a stop to their expansive plans, but only for the time being.

When we arrived in Kyrenia, obviously 40 Cdo had done a brilliant job of forcing the Turkish Army to the perimeter of Kyrenia, giving the residents some breathing space and removing any feelings of threat. The residents were given the option of leaving the island by evacuation.

I remember distinctly the TV actor Edward Woodward being very pleased to see us arrive in Kyrenia. He commented that he was very pleased to see that the British Royal Marines had arrived, and he had a tear in his eye. He was certainly thankful to have the chance of getting out of Cyprus alive, even though for some people it meant leaving their properties to the Turkish.

A lot of the residents wanted to travel out of Kyrenia

with us and fly home with the RAF, because the Turkish forces controlled the civilian airport in Nicosia.

Soon after we had secured the island and its British interests, it was decided that we should withdraw from Cyprus, letting the political process take over. But just as the advance party of 40 Cdo had departed and we had reloaded our vehicles back on board HMS Albion, the Turkish Army started to move back towards Kyrenia and did what they wanted to do all along. In the other direction they started to move towards Famagusta. It was obvious that as soon as we had departed they would move in and take control. But that was no concern of ours, even though we hated leaving a job half done. Too political for us.

I believe that some of the residents did stay in Cyprus, hopefully to protect their properties. I hope their bravery made them successful.

41 Commando was always going to be close by should the situation escalate. In the mean time it was back to Malta to settle down with our families. We had been away for just two weeks. Now we could settle for a period of family life, swimming in the afternoons down at St Georges Bay or over on the rocks at the bottom of Pembroke Ranges. This area was always very quiet and a lovely family spot. The children loved collecting sea urchins and octopus and the rocks were very clean when it came to food time.

From my point of view it was great that as a family we could pay back Marianne's lovely family in Malta for the kindness that they had shown to us in our early married days. Mind you they still enjoyed inviting us for a Maltese meal. The food was very special. The children loved spaghetti Bolognese and baked macaroni, and the latter stayed their favourite for ever. We often went to Sister Rose and Emmy's house for a meal - rabbit stew and minestrone always went down well. Occasionally Rose would accept an invitation to one of the functions at the Sergeants' Mess. That meant of course that her daughter, Carina, would be looked after by the grandparents.

Marianne's Aunty Cloty loved coming over to our house in St Andrews Barracks. She had spent years looking after her mother, so it was nice for her to have some freedom at our place, and she loved talking in English. She had never married because of her responsibilities.

Our son Marc had settled into his school in St Andrews and was part of a very good school soccer team, which contained a number of military family players. Mind you it was very difficult for these young lads playing on very hard chalk pitches.

I had now taken advantage of being overseas for the next two years by ordering a new car, duty free, one of the perks given to us by the government.

A good day out was a trip to Rabat and the Silent City. It was very eerie walking through the narrow streets with very high buildings. There were no sounds of vehicles or even people talking, although the unique properties were occupied. The occasional clip-clop of the horse-drawn Karozzin would bring you down to earth.

On the far side of the city on the perimeter were a

couple of lovely restaurants forming part of the outer city wall. We stopped and had tea and cakes. The view from that high up was stunning and overlooked the very famous RAF Ta-Qali Airfield (of the Malta story).

But now it was time to get home and prepare for our next trip away with the unit on exercise to Canada, Nova Scotia and New Brunswick. We weren't going to take any of our transport across with us, so we left a small rear party to upkeep the vehicles and to supply the rear party with their transport needs.

We were taken across to Canada, surprisingly, by HMS *Hermes*, which was dropping us off and then going on to the USA. It was a fascinating voyage in some of the roughest seas I have known, but the scenery was brilliant. The skipper had to avoid huge icebergs which could have seriously damaged even such a big ship. We saw lots of whales, a great thrill. The waves at times were coming over the flight deck, and that was some height. There were no circuits of the upper deck on days like that, or deck hockey! We could still play volleyball in the well decks, but this was a very popular sport so a booking list had to be arranged with the unit PTI.

People often ask me how you occupy your time on board Her Majesty's ships when travelling to an exercise or to combat. It depends a great deal on the size of the ship and the distance to travel. For example, when moving from Malta to Cyprus, which is a very short journey, once on board, rest, food and preparation of kit for the task in hand. On a journey from Malta to Canada, then the recreation periods, fitness training and other training must continue. Boredom must not be allowed to set in. On this particular trip, with no vehicles on board, the flight deck was nearly always available for training or recreation, if the Helicopter Squadron wasn't flying.

So what do we troops have to do on board? Mornings would normally take up military duties, inspections, weapon training, some live firing and lectures on the forthcoming exercise. After lunch the lift wells would be used for volleyball tournaments and the flight deck for deck hockey and running. Four times around the flight deck was approximately one mile.

I must tell you about the game of deck hockey, in my view the most vicious game or sport I have come across. If you can imagine 20-odd young Royal Marines with pent up emotions or frustrations, some of whom might have had grudges against the Sgt Major or anyone else, swinging a hockey stick at a puck made of ship's rope on the flight deck of a Commando Carrier steaming along at 20 knots or more in a vast ocean was a legitimate way to get revenge. The idea of the game is to get the puck into the small goal of the opposition, without taking your opponent's arms or legs or even his head off. The game normally ended up as a vicious attempt to have fun. I have seen bodies fly over the side of the ship, into the gun mounting nets or the crane mounting nets. I can't remember losing anybody, but there were always bruises and scars. I can tell you that it is no fun getting tripped up by a hockey stick when running flat out on a thick steel flight deck. But all in all, it was a very good way to get rid of excessive energy.

In the evenings there were always films, normally seen many times before, but Tom and Jerry was always a favourite. Bingo was played at the after end of the ship under cover of the flight deck overhang.

So a ten-day journey would soon go by, as long as the sea wasn't too rough. Life on board ship in general continued in a military routine and was very much like being in the barracks, except that you couldn't go home after work.

Eventually, after ten days, we arrived at Halifax, Nova Scotia. Coaches were waiting to take us to St John's, where the Canadian forces were based. There was an arrangement for us to use Canadian forces' vehicles, three-ton lorries and Jeeps, apparently on a hire basis arranged by the two governments. We had about four days to get used to the area and the vehicles. We also had a fuel bowser and a couple of water bowsers for use once we were out in the vast training area in New Brunswick. In the Second World War the area was used for the training of troops going across to Europe. The area was bigger than the UK and included towns and villages which had had to be abandoned by the residents, who were rehoused elsewhere.

Nature had taken over the whole area, which was now a dense forest with lovely lakes and some serious wildlife - brown bears, moose and huge horseflies. The cheekiest of the animals were the raccoons. They would hang around human beings and pinch anything that took their fancy.

I had just been deposited by the helicopter from
HMS Hermes to carry out a recce

Marianne enjoying a swim in Malta with the family in 1976

My daughter Isobel. Somehow she survived childhood to grow into this lovely girl

Marc and the rest of the family having a swim in Malta in 1977

One of my lads working on the ambulance in Malta in 1977

The whole family, plus, camping at Ghain Tuffieha

The battered ambulance taken on by 41 CDORM to renovate.
On behalf of the people of Malta

This is the lovely approach around the bay, to St Georges Bcks.

1977 - Our ambulance being handed over on the completion of renovation to the Maltese Government by the CO, Col Wilkins

Clothing was a favourite thing because they made nests out of items.

So it was time to move the unit to the exercise area, and a couple of journeys were needed to get all the boys and stores out there. The rifle companies were going to carry out a simulated atom bomb attack over a two-day period, and this exercise included the MT troop.

But first I had to set up a transport secure area, with a security guard who would not be involved in the exercise initially. The rest of us, including the MTO, had to build an underground three-man accommodation shelter made from items that were natural to the forest. The shelter was about three feet below ground, eight feet wide and nine feet long, and we had compo rations for two days. It was a timber frame structure, sloping down the hill and covered with a ground sheet, spruce branches and earth, with the same stuff inside as bedding. Heads were dug lower down the slope. Once the alarm came over the radio there was to be no movement outside the shelter.

This is a situation where you really have to get on with those in your shelter. Forty-eight hours doesn't sound a long time, but I can assure you that in that very close environment nerves could be shredded. There was no activity and very little one could do to relieve the boredom. Our food store was kept just outside the shelter to keep it cool. The brown bears had a very sensitive nose for food and would track it down when they were hungry. Some of these animals were huge and they weren't too afraid of humans. I saw a tin of cake which a bear had simply ripped open with its claws, and we humans struggle with a tin opener. So it was better to allow the animal to take what it wanted from outside the shelter than have him look around inside. Not nice to wake up confronted by one of those guys.

Sleep was the best way of getting time to pass quickly. Any longer than 48 hours under those conditions would drive you crazy. Torch batteries soon ran down with all the reading.

I was very glad when this experience was over. To be honest I couldn't really see the point of it, but I understand that it would have had a sort of value in the education of troops, should an atom bomb go off. So they say.

A wash and shave was the first thing on the agenda and even a sleep in the back of a truck was going to be a luxury.

The CO decided that there would be shore leave in the evenings into St John's, to the disco, so I was told to lay on three trucks every evening to get the boys to and from the town. There was no problem for the first night, but on the second we had a real issue to deal with because of a lack of professionalism by one of my drivers. All the drivers have it impressed upon them that if you have to leave your vehicle for any reason, you must immobilise it. Normally you take the keys and lock the cab. These American vehicles do not have keys, so you have to remove the rotor arm or something similar. This driver failed to do that and when he came out of the building, his vehicle had gone. He said that he had looked around for it but it could not be found.

When I learned about this I sent another vehicle out to bring the remaining lads back. I interviewed the driver and got a written statement from him, warning him that there would be a board of inquiry if the vehicle was not found. That could mean for him a court of inquiry, because the vehicle belonged to a foreign country. A board of inquiry takes some time to set up.

As luck would have it, after two days we got a message from a housing estate about twenty miles away that a military vehicle had been sighted in the woods. I took Sergeant Prescott, my senior vehicle mechanic, to the location given to us by the St John's transport people. Sure enough our vehicle was parked among the trees, deep in the woods. It appeared to both of us that whoever had taken it must have known the area very well, to park it there with hardly any damage. One sidelight was broken and there was a very small dent in the front wing. The vehicle still had fuel on board, so Sergeant Prescott checked it over and we took it back to our base.

I discussed the situation with the MTO and suggested to him that he should speak to the QM and persuade him to call off the board of inquiry. I would make sure the vehicle was repaired as good as new at no cost to the Canadians and I would deal with the driver, unless he wanted to. The MTO told me to deal with it.

I called the driver to my vehicle and gave him a good bollocking for being so unprofessional. I warned him that if the QM refused to call off the board of inquiry, he would still be in a lot of trouble. In the end it all worked out fine for everybody and a lesson was learned by all the drivers never to let it happen again.

I suggested that the MTO go back to his counterpart in St John's to see how he felt about the incident. He was happy about the way we had dealt with the situation. He acknowledged that the vehicle could have been taken by someone from the camp who just wanted to get a lift home. I think it would have been easy to find out who lived on that estate, as there couldn't have been many candidates. Anyway we didn't push it because it was our mistake.

The CO, Colonel Wilkins, was pleased that it had all been sorted to everyone's satisfaction. It was soon time to go home, so we started to move everybody back to the camp at St John's, where they were going to spend two days of rest and recuperation.

One day in the Canadian sergeants' mess, two of my SNCOs were having a drink or three together when they told me what their wives had told them about me. They had said how quiet and shy I was and how Marianne had told them she wished I wasn't so damn good and perfect. It's surprising what drink does to some people, but we had a laugh about that.

I had to make sure all the vehicles were checked for mechanical reliability and cleaned by the drivers before the handover to the Canadians. To complete the transaction we had to get the transfer documents signed and handed over to the QM. We could then leave the country knowing that there would be no comebacks or government incidents.

Most of the lads were going back by RAF VC10s, but some of us, including the CO, those who were last to leave, were on board a Hastings. This was not the most comfortable or quickest of flights, but nevertheless we were on our way home. We had to refuel at one of the UK RAF airfields. I can't remember what time we arrived back in Malta, but we made it. It was great to be home with the family, and it wasn't long before the sergeants' mess had some social events up and running.

No sooner had we got back from Canada than the unit got a signal from the promotions board wanting me to go back to the UK for promotion to RSM. I thought about it for two minutes before informing the commanding officer that in this particular case my family must come first. Having virtually just arrived in the unit, I would forgo this promotion and remain with 41 Cdo for the rest of my time in the Royal Marines.

He understood my feelings and like me, he couldn't understand why this decision to promote me hadn't been made earlier, when I was in the UK. A signal was sent declining the invitation to go back to the UK. At least the CO knew I was going to be there for the whole period of his command of 41 Cdo RM, so now I could settle down to do everything for the unit and my family.

There were quite a lot of mess functions, but it was not all good for me. Marianne's insecurity would surface every so often. I couldn't follow it.

For example, I was driving along Sliema seafront one day and the traffic was pretty busy. I checked my mirrors so that I could pull round a parked car, when Marianne said to me "Do you know her?" I really didn't know who or what she was talking about. I tried to leave it at that, but that evening at the mess function, one of her friends came across to talk to me because I was alone. Marianne was talking to some friends. From experience I had developed a listening policy rather than a talking policy on social occasions. I was apparently known as the "quiet one". I must have seemed downright rude in my efforts not to speak to women, especially Marianne's friends, but I felt I was being challenged to talk to this woman. Afterwards there was always an inquisition and I would be asked what I had been talking about.

To be accused of doing something I hadn't done really hurt. No military person would accuse another of doing something without evidence. But in your private life, especially among women, anything could be said, and was, without a shred of evidence. I always found this very difficult to understand and deal with.

But I was very proud of Marianne's beauty and it gave me a great deal of pleasure on numerous occasions to be asked "Can I dance with your wife?"
She is a wonderful, tender, loving and understanding mother, and it's a good job that she is around the children more than me, because I am too strict and disciplined. She is a beautiful wife and a good friend with just that one weakness. In due course she turned out to be an even better grandmother, so understanding and always there for the children.

The next short period away was for a helicopter training exercise from HMS *Hermes*. The pilots needed quite a lot of training and experience with the commando units, uplifting the unit and their stores and vehicles. The unit would then carry out a helicopter assault. The destination was going to be Sardinia and Corsica.

The Sea King helicopters, which had now taken over from the Wessex Fives, came in over the horizon to land on the parade ground, pick up the fighting companies and fly them out to HMS *Hermes*, which was manoeuvring just over the horizon. It would take a number of sorties to get everyone on board, then there was the stores lift, followed by the underslung vehicles; only my light vehicles were involved. The overall picture was one of the most exciting sights any young man can be involved in.

We were going to be away for one week only, because Sardinia is quite close to Malta, only a matter of hours away. My family had a smashing view of the whole thing from the balcony, and could wave me goodbye.

All my light vehicle drivers would stay with their vehicles throughout the exercise, while I and twenty lads were airlifted to the top of the target hill. There we would dig in and wait for the attack to commence.

We had a smashing view of the assault, though the helicopter blades created a lot of dust. We saw many baby tortoises in Sardinia, with lovely markings on their shells. I thought perhaps I would take a couple back for the children.

It was a very hot day for the assault, so it was fortunate that we didn't have a lot to do other than harass the fighting troops working their way inland. The climb up the assault hill was arduous in the heat, and looking down on the boys we could see how in real battle conditions they would have struggled. As it was, they came over the top to be met by a hail of fire from us. They were exhausted and thirsty, but we had plenty of water which we shared with them. They were then airlifted off the hill back to the ship. We as the enemy followed a little later.

We were then told that the ship was going on to Istanbul, not far away, to give some training to the ship's crew in entering and tying up in the very difficult quay there. This gave everyone a chance for a quick shopping run in the local market. We had only a couple of hours to buy what presents we wanted. I got a couple of very shapely onyx vases.

During that evening and overnight it was a trip back to the coast of Malta, arriving in the early hours, for the disembarkation procedure back to St Andrews. I think we must have woken up just about everybody who lived around the barrack area. Once the vehicles had been cleaned and checked over, the boys were allowed to go home for a couple of days' rest.

I don't know if it was my age, but I was finding it very difficult at home to understand my teenage daughters. The one weakness I inherited from my restricted childhood is an inability as an adult to show love and affection. I have to show it in my own way. I would much rather be strong inside and protect the ones I love and hope that they recognise that protection as love. If they don't, so be it. I will go on protecting them!

As a military man and a father, I have tried to understand women, for the sake of my daughters. I know a lot of men have tried before me and a lot more will try after me, probably all without success.

I do know they are very inconsistent and are liable to massive mood swings. Someone they liked one day they hate the next. Some women seem to live in a fantasy world, hence the love of soap operas, romantic films and books. Real life seems to be difficult for them.

I love my children, but I am not going to bend over backwards to get their love, and I will not let them prostitute themselves for the sake of their fantasies.

Young girls are like time bombs. They need handling with care, because they can explode at any time, when they engage their mouths before their brains. Before they grow out of this, they can do a lot of damage.

I love this quote: "I smile because you are my daughter. I laugh because you cannot do anything about it".

I have to laugh now at people who are against spanking and discipline. My parents whipped my backside, as did the headmaster at school. Our teachers would show their displeasure with us daily. I didn't hate them for it. I didn't have a trust issue with them because of it. I didn't fear them. Mind you I feared getting caught for doing wrong, but I respected them for their consistency. I learned what my boundaries were and I knew what would happen if I crossed them. I wasn't abused - I was disciplined.

If a policeman caught me getting up to no good, like scrumping someone's apples or such, he would clip me round the ear. If I dare say "I'm going to tell my Dad" he would take me home and tell Dad he had clipped me round the ear, and Dad would give me another one, telling me it was for letting the family down. The lack of instant discipline is the reason why kids nowadays have no respect for anyone. I could see the lack of respect arriving with my daughters. I got smacked and survived.

Back to the story. In 1976, as a sergeant major in the Royal Marines, I had never received any instructions on how to cope with two eighteen-year-olds standing to attention in my office, asking if they could have permission to take out my two daughters on a date. I was a little staggered by this approach, but I was impressed by their guts. Permission was granted, but I told them I expected the highest standard of behaviour from them. I also told them that I would not make it difficult for them, but it wouldn't be easy either.

It was at that time that I decided with other SNCOs to start a youth club for service children, to try and stem the flow of brainwashing from the schools and the media, and get them off the streets and the street mentality. We wanted to get them more interested in sport and youth activities as a group.

The old officers' mess in St George's Barracks was empty and it was a magnificent building overlooking the bay and out to sea, with tennis courts and plenty of big rooms. We managed to get together some sports equipment, a table tennis table and a pool table, and decorated a room as a snack bar so the older ones could sit and talk. We thought about self-defence classes and judo, as well as five-a-side soccer in the old tennis courts. Before long we had almost fifty members and the local children started to get interested. I wasn't sure at that point whether we should open it up to the locals, maybe at a very junior level. I was very dubious about teenagers being allowed to join because drugs were beginning to appear from Libya and elsewhere and I certainly didn't want that influence to get a hold.

At least there were plenty of big marines around to keep control of the situation and maintain a certain amount of discipline. There were occasions when groups of local lads would try to get entry, but sight of the marines soon persuaded them to leave. The youth club was very popular and very successful and it lasted a long time.

One day I was approached by a young Maltese historian who worked in the War Museum, who asked me if I could help to rebuild a 1940 Canvas Ambulance. I asked the MTO and the Commanding Officer if I could take on the project on behalf of the unit. I managed to find four MT lads who were willing to give their time to help with the rebuild. I had the vehicle mechanics on board to give their expertise.

This project was on behalf of the Maltese Government and in particular the War Museum. We were assured that there were more of these vehicles hidden away in a fortress, which might produce spare parts. The vehicle we got was the best of them all, but still in poor condition. The first task was to strip it down to the frame.

We then had to stop working on the vehicle because the unit was being sent to Cyprus, seconded to the UN to protect the areas that were under threat from the Turkish. The unit personnel were issued with blue berets, blue neckties and UN badges, which we had to get sown on before flying to Cyprus.

The RAF had a number of aircraft involved in the semi-emergency, going back and forth to the UK and Cyprus and many other countries. Once again it was goodbye to the family, but on this occasion they appeared quite happy for me to go. I think I knew the reason why – because they were looking forward to a more relaxed atmosphere with less discipline.

When we got to Limassol we took over a number of UN vehicles and I sent drivers to all the locations around the island where our troops were. The unit was well spread out with the HQ just outside Limassol.

The Commanding Officer called me in and told me he wanted me to be the Unit Air Liaison Officer, I had Colour Sergeant Joe Wren as my second-in-command; he was a very good lad and a good sportsman.

I went to the unit second-in-command, Major Syrad, to find out what my role was and what jurisdiction I had when representing the unit. He knew we were going to be out there for at least six months, so people would be moving back and forth, and he wanted everyone to have the chance to take some leave, if possible with their families. That meant flights all over the place.

First it was our job to get to know the RAF Air

Sergeants' Mess
party in Malta 1977

The Lord Chamberlain is
commanded by Her Majesty to invite

Mr and Mrs A.W.F.Collins
and Miss Denise Collins

to a Garden Party at Buckingham Palace
on Tuesday, 18th July, 1978 from 4 to 6 p.m.

Morning Dress, Uniform or Lounge Suit

Our invitation to a
Buckingham Palace
Garden Party, 1978

July 18 1978 - taken outside the
Palace, just before going in

My son Marc and I preparing to meet Lord Mountbatten
in Malta in 1977

Movements at Akrotiri, to get a feel for the movement of aircraft and to find out about the chances of flights for our lads. I decided that working at Warrant Officer level was probably the thing to do. I also liaised with the travel agency in Limassol to see if they could help. The agency's Scottish owner ran the UK end, while his Greek wife ran the Cyprus end and had the influence on the Olympus airline. This of course would mean paying for flights, so it was low on my priorities, but it was an option.

The first thing was to co-ordinate a plan of who wanted a flight, where to and when. I sent a proforma to all heads of departments so I could compile a list covering the whole unit, with dates, times, length of stay, who would pay and approvals. Leave would not commence until eight weeks into the tour and would finish at week 20. It turned out that there were almost 400 requests for flights, all within a 12-week middle period.

I went to the CO and explained the plan to him and it got his approval, so that meant an appointment with the Senior Warrant Officer at Akrotiri, and a coffee morning was arranged. When I explained the plan, he smiled and said he didn't think there would be that many spare seats available, but he would do his best. I thanked him sincerely and asked if I could liaise direct with his movement staff at Akrotiri HQ and the airport. He agreed to that, mainly I think because he didn't want to see too much of me or Joe.

We had requests for flights to India, the UK and Malta, mainly Malta. Joe and I had the freedom to move around Cyprus day and night, and we needed incoming and outgoing flights round the clock. But once the system was up and running, everyone got used to us flitting in and out.

It was a demanding job, but great fun. I managed to get a couple of kitbags full of oranges and lemons home, as the fresh fruit out there was fantastic.

We even managed to get half a dozen seats on a top secret Nimrod patrol flight backwards and forwards to Malta. These were eight-hour patrols, but it was worth it for the lads to give up eight hours of their leave before touching down in Malta. One lad got his flight to India and back to see his parents. I always had my fingers crossed that people would come back, but they did, thank goodness.

We invited the RAF staff across to our mess to have a drink with us at our base, with the kind permission of the RSM. This helped to kindle relationships and at the end of the day almost 400 got away with free flights, though one or two had to pay a little towards their flights to the UK.

Joe and I got caught up in a fracas at the rear entrance to Akrotiri, one of our main routes back to base. We managed to get out of it by some very severe cross-country driving. I really enjoyed that tour.

Soon it was all over and time for the unit to return to Malta, but first Joe and I went on a last run to Akrotiri to thank Warrant Officer Coombes for his wonderful assistance and to present him with a 41 Cdo RM shield.

On returning home, life settled down for a while. Marc was well into football now, so I was able to watch him play for the school team. He was a good young player and there were one or two other very good players in the team.

Marianne's sisters, Rose and Rita, had been visiting a lot while I was away, as did her Aunty Clotty, so I think the family were not too bored while I was away. Well - you couldn't really get bored in Malta, could you?

We heard soon after getting back from Cyprus that Lord Louis Mountbatten was coming to the island to visit the unit because 41 Cdo was the last British military unit on the island, and with its independence all traces of British dominance was being removed.

But before that, there was one place I wanted to visit on my own. It was a place I had first heard about back in 1956 as a young Marine, training here in Malta for combat in the Suez Canal - the War Graves Cemetery up on Pembroke Hill. It was a very well looked after cemetery, well worth a visit. It is the only Military War Graves Cemetery I know of which contains graves of young children and even babies. It is said that they were being treated in the military hospitals in Malta. Having been evacuated from war zones in the Med Area by military aircraft and ships, they died in the hospitals. The parents were given the option of burial in Malta or transportation back to the UK. Many of the wounded from North Africa and the Mediterranean Sea battles were taken care of in Malta's hospitals.

We all had a spot of leave in Malta, so before going back to work I wanted to spend some time with the family as possible. We decided to go camping on the beach at Ghajn Tuffieha for a couple of days with friends, and it was great fun for everybody. A couple of tents were pitched just above the water's edge and we had plenty of good food and slept with the sound of the sea just outside. I know the children enjoyed it, as they could run straight into the sea at any time. But soon it was time to go back to school, and back to work for me.

The work on the ambulance started again and it was beginning to take shape. The engine, surprisingly, was in very good condition, I believe because the vehicle had been lying on its side for some time, which allowed the oil from the sump to stay spread around the working parts, thus protecting them. It didn't take very much for the mechanics to get it running. Most of the bodywork had been done and it was looking quite smart.

The plan was to hand it over to the war museum in due course with a small ceremony. The CO agreed to attend and the Minister of Culture and the museum director were also going to be there. The people who worked on the vehicle would travel down to Valletta in the ambulance, including a nurse in full naval nurse's uniform.

But first there was the small matter of Lord Mountbatten's visit to the unit. We knew he was very fond and proud of his association with the Corps and stood up for the Royal Marines whenever there was talk of disbandment. When he arrived he visited various heads of department, with diplomatic photo sessions with the officers and SNCOs He spent time in the sergeants' mess, something he always loved doing. He was a good talker and enjoyed the jokes and banter.

While we were talking in the mess one day he asked

me how I would encourage the young people of the UK to join the Royal Marines. I told him about the scenario a few weeks before, and the extreme adrenalin rush that had occurred when the squadron of Sea King helicopters from 847 Squadron from HMS *Hermes* had suddenly appeared across the sea and on to the parade ground at St Andrew's with the whole unit on parade waiting to be transported to the ship. It was a real sight to remember, especially when the helicopters returned a short while later to pick up the underslung loads of Land Rovers and trailers. The noise and smell of the avgas fuel all added up to a wonderful memory of that scene. I said to his Lordship that any youngster watching would be influenced to join the forces. I believe my son was influenced by his experience that day, and Lord Mountbatten agreed that it was a very stimulating sight.

While talking to him I decided to be a bit cheeky and ask him a question. I asked him if he remembered the personal steward who had served with him on board HMS *Kelly*, PO Psaila, a Maltese member of the Royal Navy, who just happened to be my wife's grandfather. He thought about it for a moment and then his face lit up. "I do remember him" he said. "He served with me on other ships as well." He was too much of a gentleman to say that he didn't remember, but I believed him. When I told Aunty Cloty, who was PO Psaila's daughter, she said she had letters at home from Lord Mountbatten to his steward thanking him for taking care of him.

On occasion we as a family went across to Marsa. This

was the first area to develop grass sport areas. The Marsa golf course was a first-class course and becoming very popular. In the complex there was a cricket pitch with a grass outfield and a carpeted pitch. There were many wonderful games played there.

One game stands out in my mind, against the touring side which Freddie Truman brought across from the UK. They were ex-county players combining the games with a holiday with their families. Freddie wanted to play a game against the combined forces of Malta, and we had a choice of RAF, Royal Marines, Royal Navy, Malta Airways and the Army to choose from. Freddie had a couple of ex-England openers and he also had "the bearded wonder" - Do you remember him? The statistician scorer on BBC cricket special and radio.

It was a lovely day out, as I was selected to play for the combined services. The weather as usual was brilliant, and Marianne decided to come along for the day with the children. There were lots of facilities for them, including a swimming pool and play area. Marsa was known as the United Services Sports Club, inaugurated in 1901, and it even had a polo club across the road from the golf course.

There was also the very famous and popular Malta pony trotting club. The club had a wonderful restaurant which as an extra, specialised in a very luxurious Sunday lunch. A marvellous venue for the family.

I was very lucky to have a game of golf with the manager of Juventus soccer team and their centre forward. The team was touring Malta in their pre-season training and I just happened to be at the club when they were looking for one to make up a four.

The handover of the ambulance was a great success. I drove it to Valletta and it drove very well, without a hiccup. I must say that the boys had made a brilliant job of the rebuild, and the unit was very proud to hand over the vehicle.

It was now getting very close to our final few months in Malta as a unit and as a family, so it was essential that Marianne should spend as much time as possible with her parents and relatives. We were now in 1977, the year of the Queen's Silver Jubilee. 41 Cdo was due to disband back to the UK. We were going to leave a small rear party to tidy up and return all stores and vehicles when we were gone.

I had a wonderful accolade from my boss, the MTO Lieutenant Wally Preston, who nominated me for the Queen's Silver Jubilee Medal, while the Commanding Officer, Col Wilkins, nominated me in the Queen's Birthday Honours List. The citation read, as far as I can remember:

"I NOMINATE WO11 A W F COLLINS FOR THE MBE AND THE QUEEN'S SILVER JUBILEE MEDAL FOR OUTSTANDING SERVICE TO QUEEN AND COUNTRY, TO 41 COMMANDO RM AND THE UNITED NATIONS FORCES AND TO THE PEOPLE OF MALTA GC."

Once again it was time for the family to pack up its chattels, including my car, into boxes for dispatch by sea. This would be our last military move, because I had almost completed my pensionable service. Those 22 years seemed to have gone in less time than it has taken to write about it.

As far as the story goes this was the end of the "Cockney Commando", because he was now going to be plain Mr Collins. But I think one more memory can be added to the story as a finale. On arriving back in the UK, I was discharged from the Royal Marines in Poole Dorset. Then one day, after all the formalities of saying goodbye and seeing the Commanding Officer, I received a personal report from the Commandant General Royal Marines, thanking me for the loyal and devoted service to the Marines. In addition I received an invitation from Her Majesty the Queen which read: "The Lord Chamberlain is commanded by her majesty to invite Mr and Mrs A. W. F. Collins and Miss Denise Collins to a garden party at Buckingham Palace on Tuesday 18th July 1978."

It was a lovely day out and a further experience to add to the memoirs of the Cockney Commando.